PILGRIMS & PROPHETS

Edmond Cullinan is a priest of the Diocese of Waterford and Lismore. His doctoral thesis was on Contemplation in the Theology of St Thomas Aquinas. He has wide experience as a lecturer, pastor and author. He has lectured in systematic theology, liturgy and the history of spirituality. His experience as a parish priest has given him a particular insight into how theology, liturgy and spirituality are lived in practice. He is interested in spirituality and liturgy in an Irish context and has written extensively on these topics.

PILGRIMS & PROPHETS

Biblical and Celtic Spirituality

Edmond Cullinan

VERITAS

Published 2015 by
Veritas Publications
7–8 Lower Abbey Street
Dublin 1, Ireland
publications@veritas.ie
www.veritas.ie

ISBN 978 1 84730 590 9

10 9 8 7 6 5 4 3 2 1

A catalogue record for this book is available from the British Library.

Cover designed by Barbara Croatto, Veritas
Printed in the Republic of Ireland by SPRINT-print Ltd, Dublin

Veritas books are printed on paper made from the wood pulp of managed forests. For every tree felled, at least one tree is planted, thereby renewing natural resources.

In memory of my mother Enda
(1918–2014)

And for my aunt Eileen

CONTENTS

FOREWORD

As a wonderful spiritual director, Pope Francis has often referred to the importance of spirituality. For instance, in *Evangelii Gaudium* (The Joy of the Gospel), he writes that people need to find in the Church a spirituality that can offer 'healing and liberation, and fill them with life and peace, while at the same time summoning them to fraternal communion and missionary fruitfulness' (n. 89).

I congratulate the author, a priest of the Diocese of Waterford and Lismore, for providing us with a work that responds to the pope's encouragement of robust pathways in spirituality. It helps us, as the author says in his introduction, to rediscover, not least within the Irish tradition, how 'spirituality is not just about prayer, or those activities that we tend to think of as spiritual, but it about the whole of life'.

In exploring various approaches to spirituality, the author clarifies how in a genuine Christian spirituality, union with God, fraternal communion and mission are very much interlinked. Neither a unilateral focus on inner individual mindfulness nor mere external social activism satisfies. He wants to assist us as we respond to the practical question: 'How can we cultivate spirituality in our lives?'

In recalling the history of Christianity in Ireland, this book provides us with perspectives to face the challenges of today. The forms and structures of Church life have changed greatly over the centuries, but the spiritual insight and practices have continued in various guises. As the author deftly highlights, in many ways we can see the continuing legacy of the Irish monastic tradition as a constant throughout the years in the various waves of initiatives in prayer, learning and mission.

A striking feature of this book is the riches it offers in its presentation of many inspiring prophetic figures that have lived the spiritual life deeply, from ancient times right up to our own times. The light, life and wisdom that these women and men exhibited in the course of their own life still continues to shine years, centuries and indeed millennia afterwards.

We have much to learn from them about how to be pilgrims along life's journey in a way that fulfils us. That's why there are many points in this book at which the reader will be stopped in their tracks and prompted to meditate on what is written. It will become obvious to the reader of this text that it is the fruit of many years' reading, reflecting and synthesising on the part of its author – a teacher of theology, a liturgist and pastor. It pulls many elements together: history and holiness; liturgy and spirituality; hierarchy and charism; contemplation and moral theology.

It has been said that in the recent past, Christian faith was practised in Ireland in a rigorous fashion, whereas today we risk falling into laxism, an 'anything goes' approach. This book draws upon the best of the Christian tradition in a way that helps us to re-read the Church's teaching in terms of wisdom for living. This is a far cry from reducing the spiritual life to simply listing off what is permitted and what is forbidden, or dumbing it down to a worthless laxity.

In its truest sense, a Christian spirituality is a spirituality of incarnation, the Word becoming flesh, Good News becoming everyday life. Such spirituality is nothing less than our sharing in the life of the Trinity and living this life together in the communion of our love for one another.

I hope that many will benefit from the encounters with the many pilgrims, prophets and wise people that the author opens up for us in these pages. We are indebted to him. They have left a trail of light to inspire us.

Bishop Brendan Leahy
Limerick
Feast of the Presentation of the Lord in the Temple
2 February 2015

ACKNOWLEDGEMENTS

There has been a great growth in interest in spirituality in recent years. The subject has been revitalised especially by what the French call *ressourcement*, that is, by going back to the sources. These are the Bible and the lived tradition of the Church, especially as it has been expressed in the lives of the saints. The topics that I discuss in the present volume are a personal selection from these sources. The result is a combination of research and my own reflections. I hope these will be of interest to the reader.

I have made use of two pieces that I published previously. In both cases I have considerably revised and adapted them. In Chapter Three, 'The Wisdom Tradition: Learning from the Experience of the Community', I have made use of 'The Wisdom Tradition and Moral Theology', which appeared in *Hallel*, Vol. 31, No. 1 (2006), edited by an tAthair Ciarán Ó Sabhaois OCSO. In Chapter Five, 'St John's Spirituality of the Incarnation', I have made use of 'Johannine Spirituality', which appeared in *Having Life in His Name* (Dublin: Veritas, 2011), edited by Brendan Leahy and Séamus O'Connell. In both cases I thank the editors for their encouragement to rework and reuse the material.

I am very grateful to Bishop Brendan Leahy for writing the foreword. I also wish to thank Bishop William Lee for his encouragement and support.

A number of people have helped me in my research by providing me with material and advice. I want to thank the following most sincerely: Br Eoin de Bhaldraithe OCSO, Bolton Abbey; Sr Carol Breslin MMM, Medical Missionaries of Mary, Booterstown; Fr Seán Casey PP, Killoe; Ms Niamh Collins, archivist, Columbans, Navan; Fr Raymond Collins OP, Dominicans, Waterford; Eibhlín Bean Uí Dhonnachadha, An Rinn; Fr Michael Kennedy PP, New Inn; Dr Frank Lawrence, Music Department, UCD; Dr Michael Mullins PP, Ballybricken; Fr Flor O'Callaghan OSA, Augustinians, Dungarvan; and Fr Malachy Smyth SSC, Columbans, Navan.

Finally, I would like to thank Veritas Publications, especially Ms Donna Doherty, commissioning editor, and Mr Daragh Reddin, managing editor, for bringing the book to its readers.

Edmond G. Cullinan
Carrick-on-Suir
Feast of Our Lady of Lourdes
11 February 2015

INTRODUCTION

WHAT IS SPIRITUALITY?

Every human being has the capacity to relate to God. There is at the core of every person an empty space that can only be filled by God. This is what the Bible calls the heart. Saint Augustine put it rather well when he said: 'You have made us for yourself, O Lord, and our hearts are restless until they rest in you.'[1] This spiritual core of the person is developed by religion and becomes a lived experience, a life of faith.

Spirituality is not just about prayer, or those activities that we tend to think of as spiritual, but about life in its entirety. There is no dichotomy between religion and spirituality. The purpose of religion is to promote spirituality. When religious practices lose their meaning or simply become outward observances divorced from faith, then religion no longer promotes spirituality and is dead.

Spirituality takes different forms depending on the particular faith formation one receives. Christian spirituality is the lived experience of faith in God, Father, Son and Holy Spirit. All Christian spirituality is based on the teaching of Christ and so will have the same basic themes in common. However, because we are dealing with lived experience, it is possible to have different starting points and emphases. Each Christian tradition has its own spirituality. Indeed, each of the great traditions is so rich that it contains many spiritualities. So, for instance, under the general heading of Catholic spirituality we find Benedictine spirituality, Ignatian spirituality and so on. Together they provide a rich treasury of approaches to finding God in our lives.

In this book I want to explore various approaches to spirituality. As I am coming at this question from an Irish context, I am particularly interested in what our Irish tradition has to contribute, but I do not confine myself to this. I begin with early Irish monasticism. The high crosses, round towers and other artefacts continue to interest and inspire us, but does anything remain of the spirituality of the people who left these treasures behind? Chapter One explores the continuity of monastic life in Ireland through the different forms it has taken.

Chapter Two explores the tradition of pilgrimage, an aspect of Irish spirituality that is very much alive. The idea of pilgrimage, *peregrinatio* in Latin, encompasses the ideas of exile and mission.

An aspect of Gaelic culture that has, perhaps, been neglected by scholars is the oral tradition of wisdom, which is passed on in the form of proverbs. There is also a wisdom tradition in the Bible and a wisdom tradition in the life of the Church. Chapter Three explores this tradition.

The hierarchy, the priesthood and the various structural elements insure the authenticity of the Christian message and the continuity of the Church of today with that of the apostles. Complementing the structural aspect of the Church is the charismatic element represented by prophetic figures such as St Francis of Assisi and St Teresa of Ávila. Chapter Four explores the prophetic tradition. I give some examples of how the charism of prophecy continues to be a gift to the Church.

Saint John's Gospel seems to have been the favourite Gospel in the early Irish Church. The Church in Gaul was an important influence: the early missionaries who brought the Gospel to Ireland came from there or spent some time there; Lyons was the major centre in Gaul, with its first bishop being St Irenaeus who had been taught by St Polycarp, who in turn had been taught by St John. Chapter Five explores the spirituality to be found in the Gospel and Epistles of John.

Having looked at various themes in spirituality from a theoretical perspective, in the final chapter I ask the practical question: 'How can we cultivate spirituality in our lives?' The liturgy, spiritual reading and prayer are the principal means that I propose for cultivating spirituality. I also recommend getting involved in some Christian community or group. I conclude with some suggestions on what the characteristics of a contemporary Irish spirituality might be.

NOTE

1. Saint Augustine, *Confessions,* 1, 1.

CHAPTER ONE

WHATEVER HAPPENED TO EARLY IRISH MONASTICISM?

Origins of Monasticism

Monasticism as a movement associated with the desert began with St Antony of Egypt (251–356).[1] As a young man he renounced his inheritance and went into the desert to be alone with God. Another desert father, St Arsinius, prayed to be led in the way of salvation and heard the reply: 'Flee the world, be silent and pray always.'[2] This approach typifies the monasticism of the desert. After a while people became aware of these hermits and went to them for advice. Others settled near them in order to imitate their way of life. In this way, solitude led to community.

Saint Pachomius (c. 290–346) gave a rule to these communities and so gave rise to coenobitic monasticism. The *coenobium* or community was gathered around an *abba* (father) or *amma* (mother) in order to avail of his or her spiritual guidance. The monks or nuns were still essentially hermits who had come together to help one another in their search for God. Community was secondary to the desire to be alone with God. The monasticism of the desert includes both the way of life of hermits (eremitical) and that of monks living in community (coenobitic).

The ideal of desert monasticism spread rapidly. An early centre from which it spread in the west was the island of Lérins in the Bay of Cannes in Provence where

St Honoratus (c. 350–c. 430) founded a monastery. There is a belief that St Patrick spent some time there.[3] Each monastery was ruled by an abbot or abbess. While the founder lived, there was no need for written regulations, but after the founder had died some kind of document encapsulating his or her teaching was found to be useful. In this way many monastic rules appeared, some written by the founders themselves, others by their successors and ascribed to them retrospectively. Saint Benedict of Nursia (c. 480–c. 550) wrote his rule towards the end of his life for the three monasteries he had founded. It was based on his experience as abbot for many years and also came at the end of a long period of development in the monastic experiment. For centuries it was one rule among many, but eventually became the accepted norm for monasticism in the west.

There was also another kind of monasticism, which comprised similarly of a search for God but had a different starting point. It started with community: with the sharing of a common life. God is to be found in community, in mutual love and in love of neighbour. The classical expression of this kind of monasticism is to be found in the Rule of St Augustine. The Rule states the ideal as follows: 'Before all else, live together in harmony, being of one mind and one heart on the way to God.'[4] This ideal is based on the model of the Jerusalem community described in the Acts of the Apostles.[5] It could be applied to communities involved in an active apostolate and also to those devoted to contemplation. This type of monasticism is probably older than that of the desert. It developed out of the communities of virgins. Saint Augustine wrote his Rule for a community of women who asked him for guidance (though the communities he founded were of men.)

The earliest form of the religious life is that of the virgins: women who took a vow of celibacy and dedicated their lives to prayer and the service of the Christian community. They are alluded to by St Paul[6] and mentioned in such early documents as the *Apostolic Tradition* attributed to St Hippolytus.[7] They are not usually seen as monastic, because they did not withdraw from the world, but continued to live in their own homes. However, by the fourth century, and probably earlier, there were communities of virgins.

Communal monasticism usually began in an urban setting and, as in the case of Augustine, started with a group of friends. The leader (*praepositus*) is to serve the community in love.[8] He or she is to be an example, but there is no mention of spiritual guidance as in the case of the *abba* or *amma* of the desert tradition. For convenience, we may call it Augustinian type monasticism, although there were other exponents besides St Augustine, particularly St Basil.

A third kind of monasticism may be mentioned, which is really a variation on the second. This arises where a bishop organises his clergy into a monastic community. Again we have the example of St Augustine. Monasticism was a lay movement originally and Augustine's community at Tagaste (388) was a lay community. The community he set up at Hippo in 391 was also of lay people, although he himself had been ordained a presbyter at this time. When he became bishop (395) he set up another house for clerics.[9] We may call this 'ecclesiastical monasticism' as it was at the service of the local Church. Other examples are the communities set up by St Martin of Tours and St Caesarius of Arles.

Monasticism in Ireland

Monasticism has been a feature of Irish Christianity from very early times. Saint Patrick tells us in his *Confessio* that the sons and daughters of the Irish were dedicating themselves as monks and virgins of Christ.[10] Saint Patrick promoted this enthusiastically. It was a sign of the vigour and authenticity of his new communities. Most of these religious continued to live at home, like the virgins of the early Church on the continent. Indeed, some were slaves, so they had no choice about where they lived, but Patrick still championed their right to consecrate themselves to Christ. It appears from later literature that St Patrick also set up communities of nuns in association with some of the churches he founded. The mention of monks suggests that there were also male celibates, some of whom may have been clergy. The communities of nuns are often associated with bishops and may have provided bases from which the bishops worked. They were also to the fore in caring for others.[11]

The monasticism promoted by St Patrick is clearly similar to that formulated by St Augustine. The monastic movement that came from the desert made its way from Gaul to Britain and arrived in Ireland in the sixth century. Among the founders of the early sixth century are St Enda of Aran, St Buíte of Monasterboice, St Ciarán of Clonmacnois and St Brigid of Kildare. The later sixth century saw a proliferation of monasteries in many parts of Ireland. This was the period of charismatic founders like St Finnian of Clonard, St Comgall of Bangor and St Columba who founded Durrow and Derry. Saint Kevin of Glendalough and St Carthage of Lismore belong to the early seventh century.

Pre-Benedictine monasticism on the continent was quite varied in character. The two main traditions inevitably influenced each other. Each founder also had his or her particular approach to the monastic life, which added to the distinctiveness of every monastery. The Irish monasteries were also quite varied in character. Some of the monasteries began with hermits or ascetics who wanted to live a solitary life, but then attracted followers, and so a monastic settlement grew up. Glendalough would appear to have started in this way with St Kevin. Other monasteries, like Lismore, became great centres of learning. Some, like Sceilig Mhichíl off the coast of Kerry, were places of flight from the world. Others were more pastoral in orientation. Clonmacnois was literally on the main crossroads of Ireland and became the centre of a large settlement.

A characteristic of early Irish monasticism was a strong devotion to the founder. It was the founder who gave each particular community its distinct personality. The successor was called the *comharba* and was believed to inherit the charism of the founder in a manner analogous to that of the Pope as the successor of St Peter.[12] Monasteries with the same founder formed a family or *paruchia*.[13] The abbot or abbess of the main house was the *comharba* and his or her authority was recognised in the dependent houses. For instance, the abbot of Iona was the *Comharba Choluim Cille* until Iona had to be partially evacuated in the ninth century due to Viking attacks. Kells became the seat of the *comharba*, when the Iona monks fled there, bringing the famous book with them, subsequently known as the Book of Kells.[14] In the twelfth century the abbot of Derry became the *comharba* and went on a visitation around the other Columban monasteries collecting tribute.[15]

In the eighth century a new group of monks appeared in Ireland. These were the *Céli Dé*. The founders of this group were St Maelruain of Tallaght and St Dublittir of Finglas. They in turn appear to have been influenced by the three closely associated monasteries of Lismore, Dairinis and Derrynaflan. They were a very influential group and spread to other centres such as Armagh and Clonmacnois.[16] The surviving monastic literature in Irish comes from this milieu. This includes the monastic rules, like the Rule of Carthage retrospectively attributed to St Carthage, but in fact giving us an accurate picture of life in a ninth century monastery.[17]

The Rule of Carthage outlines the duties of the different persons living in the monastery. Among them are the bishop, the abbot, the priest, the soul-friend, the monk and the *Céli Dé*. The duties of the monk are the usual virtues of self-control and good behaviour. The duties of the *Céli Dé* that are listed have to do mainly with the celebration of the Office, and it is clear that some were in holy orders and celebrated Mass. The distinction between the *Céli Dé* and the monk seems to be similar to that which obtained between choir monks and *conversi* in the later Middle Ages.[18]

A number of monasteries in Ireland were examples of what I have called ecclesiastical monasticism. In these cases, what started out as episcopal centres developed into monasteries. Armagh is a good example, as are the other centres traditionally regarded as having been founded as bishoprics by St Patrick or by his companions, such as Ardagh, Elphin, Clogher and Connor. Emly and Ardmore were also in existence before the monastic movement took off in Ireland. On the continent the bishop normally lived in a city. As there were no cities in Ireland before the coming of the Vikings, it was natural that he should live in a monastery or that a monastic settlement should grow up around him. A monastery of this kind would have a strong pastoral orientation.

It has often been asserted that the Irish Church became entirely monastic in character.[19] That view has been challenged recently.[20] The details of the relationship between bishops and monasteries need not concern us here, as our interest is in the spirituality of the monasteries. Throughout the period, from the fifth to the eleventh century, bishops continued to function, even if in some cases their role was mainly sacramental. A close relationship between bishops and monasteries was not unique to Ireland, although the form it took was unusual. During this period on the continent and in Britain, many bishops were themselves monks and enlisted monks to help them in pastoral and missionary work. A good example is St Gregory the Great (c. 540–604), who had been a monk before becoming pope, and sent forty monks, led by Augustine, to Britain on a mission to the Anglo-Saxons.

Perhaps the use of the term 'monastery' is a bit misleading for the modern reader. We tend to think of a monastery as an impressive complex of buildings, joined together and inhabited by a community of either men or women with religious vows. The typical early Irish monastery was comprised of separate small timber or wattle-and-daub thatched houses in an enclosure made by an earthwork. It usually had a high cross and may have had a round tower. It was inhabited by monks or nuns, but the community of the 'monastery' also included lay people, single and married with families who lived in the area surrounding the central enclosure.

The Spirituality of Early Irish Monasticism

Most of the Irish monasteries are clearly in the tradition of desert monasticism. Others show an affinity with the Augustinian type in that the ideal of community was central. This is especially the case in communities of women. Not much is known for certain about St Brigid of Kildare, but the legends that have accrued around her point to a person of practical charity. The fact that so many monasteries became Augustinian in the twelfth century points to the likelihood that they already had a broadly similar spirituality.

The spirituality of early Irish monasticism is characterised by an intense spirit of prayer. The monk was to pray at all times, whether alone in his cell, or in common with the community. They prayed with the body as well as with the mind and heart: when reciting the psalms, it was the practice to prostrate oneself after each psalm, or after each group of three psalms in the longer offices. Another practice was the cross-vigil. This was praying, sometimes for lengthy periods, with arms outstretched in the form of a cross. This is usually interpreted as a penitential exercise, but it was also a mystical identification with Christ crucified.

The Irish were particularly devoted to the recitation of the psalms. *The Antiphonary of Bangor* and the *Rule of the Monks of St Columbanus*, both from the seventh century, show that they celebrated the Liturgy of the Hours and that the vigil office during the night was particularly long. *The Rule of the Célí Dé* and the *Rule of Tallaght* prescribed the recitation of the entire Psalter every day. The *Antiphonary* also contains hymns, including the beautiful '*Sancti venite*', the oldest known communion hymn in Latin. The literature that comes from the *Célí Dé* movement also shows that the Mass had a central place in the lives of the monks. They are encouraged to receive Holy Communion on Sundays and Thursdays. The Stowe Missal, the Derrynaflan chalice and paten and the Faddan More Psalter all come from this milieu.[21]

Solitude was valued by the early Irish monks and nuns. Each religious lived in an individual cell. There was also often a *díseart*, a place where one could retreat to in order to be completely alone. Columbanus had a cave some distance from the monastery at Bobbio to which he used to go for long periods. Solitude is the other side of community: one can only give oneself to others in community if one can also be alone. Solitude is obviously conducive to silence, but silence is also of value when monks or nuns live in community. Encouraged in the monastic literature, silence was the precondition for prayer and also for recollection – that gathering together of oneself so characteristic of the contemplative. It was also seen as a way of avoiding gossip and murmuring.

A spirit of penance was part of Irish monastic spirituality. The Irish approach to penance was far less severe and much more pastorally effective than the approach adopted on the continent at the time. There people who had committed grave public sins were enrolled in the Order of Penitents and often had to spend years before being readmitted to full communion with the Church. In Ireland there was no Order of Penitents, but there was a recognition that we are all sinners in need of the medicine of God's mercy. One could say that in Ireland everyone was a penitent. It was in Ireland that the practice of frequent confession and absolution was pioneered. The penances imposed may seem severe to us, but in fact the approach set out in the *Penitentials* offered hope to sinners, whereas the more rigorous canonical system used in other places often meant that people simply gave up and went from bad to worse.

Asceticism was seen as part of being a Christian. This was true everywhere at the time. Throughout the Christian world people fasted on Wednesdays, Fridays, during Lent and in the period before Christmas, which would eventually become Advent. Meat was a luxury item and not part of most people's everyday diet. When seen in this broader context the regime in Irish monasteries does not seem particularly severe. Some individuals, in their enthusiasm, carried things a bit further, but that happened everywhere. Asceticism was united to prayer and helped to concentrate the mind. This can still be seen in Lough Derg. One way of practising detachment was to go on pilgrimage.

Pastoral involvement was part of Irish monasticism. As mentioned above, some of the monasteries began as secular churches with bishops and clergy, so it was natural that they would continue to provide pastoral services. There was also a missionary aspect. This may have begun as going on pilgrimage, but the monks tended to respond to whatever needs they found when they arrived in a new place.

The early Irish monasteries were centres of learning. The preservation of ancient manuscripts, the copying of books and their elaborate ornamentation is something for which they are famous. The monasteries not only preserved the Bible and the works of Christian writers, but they preserved secular works as well. It was the monks who committed the ancient legends such as the *Táin Bó Cuallainge* and the *Fiannaíocht* to print. Centres such as Clonmacnois and Lismore had hundreds of students, many of whom came from Britain and the continent.

The Irish monasteries were also centres of hospitality. Saint Bede in his *Ecclesiastical History* is high in his praise of the Irish monasteries, both for their learning and for their hospitality. He says that many English folk went to Ireland to pursue religious studies or to enter the monastic life. Bede says that the Irish 'welcomed them all kindly, and without asking for any payment, provided them with daily food, books and instruction'.[22]

Irish Monasticism on the Continent: St Columbanus

Saint Columbanus was born in Leinster and spent most of his early life as a monk in the monastery of St Comgall in Bangor in what is now County Down. He was a good scholar and became head of the monastic school. When he expressed the desire to become a pilgrim for Christ, Comgall was reluctant to let him go, but eventually agreed. At the age of forty-five, Columbanus set sail for Gaul with twelve companions. This was in the year 590 or 591.[23] After some time travelling around, they settled in the Vosges Mountains in Burgundy. Columbanus's first foundation at Annegray was soon full and it became necessary to establish a second house at Luxeuil and a third at Fontaine. All three were within a few miles of each other and under Columbanus's authority. Luxeuil became the main centre and it is believed that there were over two hundred monks in the three houses together. Saint Columbanus is remembered as a great missionary, but he was first and foremost a monk. He spent twenty years in Luxeuil as abbot. His monasteries were effective in reviving Christianity in the surrounding areas and also in spreading his particular kind of monasticism.

Saint Columbanus left two rules: the Rule of the Monks (*Regula Monachorum*) and the Community Rule (*Regula Coenobialis*). Reading these, one gets the impression that the regime in his monasteries was very harsh. However, that does not seem to have put off the large number of young men who came to enter his monasteries. The idealism of Columbanus seems to have had quite an appeal. The demanding rule may not have seemed so severe to the enthusiastic young Frankish monks. They were not coming from a pampered background, but rather were just emerging from barbarism. Saint Columbanus was a rugged frontiersman who obviously had great appeal to these young people.

As the enthusiasm of youth faded – as it does for communities as well as for individuals – it became necessary to temper Columbanus's rigour with the more humane measures prescribed by St Benedict. The Rule of St Benedict became the classical expression of western monasticism because of Benedict's profound understanding of human nature. He too had been very harsh as a young abbot, so much so that his first community tried to poison him, but he wrote his rule when he was old and had learned from long experience. In the seventh century the Rule of St Benedict was disseminated through the monasteries founded by St Columbanus and the many daughter houses acquired by them, and the two rules combined. During the Carolingian Reform in the ninth century the Columbanian monasteries were to the fore in promoting the Benedictine Rule.[24]

Saint Columbanus was a controversial figure during his time in the Frankish lands. He clashed with the bishops on a number of occasions on issues such as the dating of Easter and the discipline of penance. In 610 he ran into trouble with the ruling royal family, when he denounced their immoral lifestyle, and was expelled from their territory. Now he really became a wanderer for Christ. With his Irish companions, he set out to return to Ireland from Nantes, but the ship on which they were to sail was prevented from putting to sea by a storm. They interpreted this as a sign from God that they were not to go back to Ireland, and so instead they travelled eastwards and then up the Rhine to Lake Constance. They settled at Bregenz for over a year and preached to the Alemanni, a Germanic tribe. In 612 they encountered such hostility that Columbanus decided that they would move again. Gall, one of the original twelve who had come from Ireland with Columbanus, was proficient in the local language and stayed behind in order to continue the work of evangelisation.[25] His foundation became the monastery and city of Sankt Gallen. Columbanus and the others journeyed over the Alps into Lombardy and stayed in Milan for some months in 613. The local ruler then gave Columbanus a site with a ruined church dedicated to St Peter in the mountains seventy miles to the south. This was to become the famous abbey of Bobbio. Saint Columbanus died in a little hermitage a short distance from the monastery on 23 November 615.

Six letters written by St Columbanus survive. Three of them are to popes. His letter to Pope Boniface IV is the oldest extant expression of Irish identity. 'For all we Irish, inhabitants of the world's edge, are disciples of Saints Peter and Paul and of all the disciples who wrote the sacred canon by the Holy Spirit.'[26] His *Letter to a Young Disciple* shows us the kind of principles by which he lived himself:

> Be friendly with men of honour, stiff with rascals, gentle to the weak, firm to the stubborn, steadfast to the proud, humble to the lowly ... Be timely in fasting, timely in the night-offices, discreet in duty, persistent in study, unshaken in turmoil, joyful in suffering, valiant in the cause of truth, cautious in time of strife.[27]

A series of St Columbanus's sermons survive. These were probably written and delivered during St Columbanus's sojourn in Milan.[28] The thirteenth sermon in particular reveals the more mystical side of Columbanus. This is a meditation on the Eucharist in which Columbanus talks about being wounded by love and thirsting for the living water which is Christ himself.[29]

The monasteries founded by St Columbanus on the continent quickly became local communities, but retained a strong devotion to their founder. Some of them enjoyed a continuous history longer than any monastery in Ireland. Luxeuil in Burgundy continued until the French Revolution; Bobbio in Italy survived until it was suppressed by Napoleon; Sankt Gallen in Switzerland, founded by Columbanus's companion Gall, was secularised in the mid-nineteenth century. All of these famous Irish foundations became Benedictine over time, but undoubtedly retained much of their Columbanian spirit. Even today there is a strong awareness of the Irish connection in Luxeuil, Bobbio and Sankt Gallen, with the library in Sankt Gallen still holding a very fine collection of Irish manuscripts as well as the oldest copy of the Rule of St Benedict. The former monastic churches are still used as places of worship for the local communities.

The Twelfth-Century Reform

None of the monasteries of pre-Norman Ireland has survived to the present day. However, it is worth asking the question whether anything survives of their spiritual heritage. The 'Twelfth-Century Reform' is often seen as bringing an end to early Irish monasticism and replacing it with religious orders from the continent. This is an over-simplification. The pre-twelfth century Irish Church was not isolated from continental influences. This can be seen, for instance, in the early ninth century Stowe Missal which contains elements from various places. We tend to think of the sea as a barrier, but in Antiquity and in the Middle Ages the seas were the great highways. By the twelfth century great monasteries like Lismore had absorbed many continental and English influences. Frank Lawrence has shown that in the area of liturgical chant, the monks of Lismore were familiar with material from Benedictine monasteries in Normandy as well as from the English cathedrals of Winchester and Canterbury.[30] No doubt they were also familiar with the Rule of St Benedict, but this does not mean that they had become Benedictines. They probably saw it as another source of monastic wisdom alongside the Rule of Carthage and the writings of Cassian, St Augustine and St Basil. The tenth and eleventh centuries had been periods of decline. The time was right for the movement known as the Twelfth-Century Reform. This movement affected all aspects of Church life, including monasticism. One of the major figures associated with it was St Malachy, although the movement had started before he got involved.

There were two important developments in religious life on the continent in the eleventh century: the emergence of the Augustinians and the Cistercians. Both were to play an important part in the renewal of the Irish Church in the twelfth century. As mentioned above, the Rule of St Augustine was written by the Bishop of Hippo at the end of the fourth century and was already well known in religious circles, but religious life had been dominated by the Rule of St Benedict since the ninth century. However, in the eleventh century the Rule of St Augustine was rediscovered, so to speak, and took off as a basis for community life and was adopted by many groups, male and female, lay and clerical.[31]

Among the groups being set up under the Rule of St Augustine were canons regular. They were basically communities of priests engaged in the usual pastoral and liturgical priestly duties, many of which were set up by bishops. They were indeed examples of what I have called ecclesiastical monasticism. They did not belong to a single order, but each house was autonomous and usually under the authority of the bishop. By the twelfth century, orders or congregations of canons regular were emerging on the continent. Groups like the Norbertines or the Arrouaisians began with a single community and went on to found others which shared the same constitutions as well as the basic rule.

Saint Malachy was familiar with both the older forms of monastic life surviving in Ireland and with religious life on the continent. In the 1120s Malachy spent some time in Lismore, which was a major religious centre at the time. After that he was put in charge of the ancient Irish monastery of Bangor. He renewed the community there with the help of religious from the monastery of St Peter and St Paul in Armagh which, apparently, had already adopted the Rule of St Augustine, making them the first such community in Ireland.[32] Malachy's earliest contacts with Augustinians from outside Ireland were with those from Guisborough in Yorkshire.[33] There were many houses of Augustinian canons regular in the north of England.

During his travels on the continent, on his way to and from Rome to visit the pope, Malachy visited Clairvaux, one of the new Cistercian foundations where St Bernard was abbot. He also visited Arrouaise in Flanders where there was a community of canons regular who followed the Rule of St Augustine, with their own constitutions that placed an emphasis on contemplation. Saint Malachy introduced both these orders to Ireland. The first Cistercian house was at Mellifont, founded in 1142, and the first Arrouaisian community was at Louth, founded around the same time.

In both cases he had Irishmen trained by the respective orders.[34]

Clairvaux was a daughter house of Cîteaux in Burgundy, where a new monastery was founded in 1098 with the intention of returning to a simpler way of life based on a stricter observance of the Rule of St Benedict. One cannot avoid the impression that the Cistercians owe much to the inspiration of St Columbanus, who had such an impact on the Burgundy region. Although the Cistercians were a new order, St Malachy must have felt that their spirituality would fit in with his project of renewing religious life in Ireland. In this he was correct; their idealism and asceticism appealed to the Irish spirit. Mellifont had seven daughter houses by 1171.[35] There were also some Benedictine communities like Erenagh near Down which later became Cistercian.[36] Marie Therese Flanagan has shown that there was more continuity between Irish monastic culture and the new Cistercian foundations than had been previously thought.[37]

It is interesting that Malachy saw the need for both Cistercians and Augustinians. He had wanted to join the Cistercians himself, but was refused permission to do so by Pope Innocent II. It seems obvious that he would have contented himself with introducing the Cistercians, but he saw the need for another, more pastorally oriented order as well. The Rule of St Augustine was already making headway in Ireland. Saint Malachy encouraged this trend and used the Augustinian rule as a template for reconstituting the monasteries that he reformed. These included Louth, Bangor and Downpatrick. It may be surmised that he detected a certain affinity between the older monasteries and the Rule of St Augustine, especially as followed by the Canons of Arrouaise.

A generation later than St Malachy, but also straddling both old and new, St Lorcán Ó Tuathail grew up in the ancient monastery of Glendalough. He was abbot there from around 1150 until 1161 when he became Archbishop of Dublin. Lorcán also promoted the Augustinian Canons of Arrouaise. During his time as abbot he founded St Saviour's Priory in Glendalough. When he became Archbishop of Dublin he installed a community of Augustinian Canons in Christ Church Cathedral and also founded the monastery of All Hallows on the site of the present Trinity College.[38] These three varied examples show the adaptability of the Augustinian Rule. In Glendalough the canons were in a contemplative setting, in Christ Church they were the clergy of a busy metropolitan cathedral, and in All Hallows they were in an urban monastic situation.

It is estimated that during the twelfth century and the early decades of the thirteenth, 181 houses of Augustinian Canons were set up. Over forty convents of Augustinian nuns or canonesses were also established.[39] There were some 'double houses' like Clonard where a convent of women was adjacent to a monastery for men and they shared the same church. This had been a feature of some early Irish monasteries like that of St Brigid in Kildare. Another example is St Hilda's in Whitby in the north of England, where there was a strong Irish influence. Most of these Augustinian foundations were not new communities, but examples of early Irish monasteries reinventing themselves.

The Twelfth-Century Reform in Ireland was somewhat like Vatican II, in that one could speak of the Church before and after this event. One could point out changes in the particular forms of liturgy or religious life, but there was a basic continuity as well. It was the same Church. The major change in the twelfth century was the setting up of the dioceses. Religious life became more structured. There were new communities. In some places the old blended into the new and in some cases the old forms continued to exist beside the new. The Augustinian Abbot of Lorrha in north Tipperary, Gillaruadáin Ó Macán, was still being styled 'Comharba Ruadáin' when his name was inscribed on the shrine of the Stowe Missal in the mid-fourteenth century.[40] Traditional monasticism continued in Derry[41] and there was a community of *Célí Dé*, with a prior, in Armagh up to the sixteenth century.[42]

The Mendicants

One of the basic concepts in the Rule of St Benedict is that of stability. This is not mainly about staying in one place, although it does include that. It is about committing oneself to a particular community and it means sticking at the work of self-conversion. Saint Benedict deplored the practice of moving about from one monastery to another. Some monks thought that if they had problems in one community, they could move somewhere else and do better, but in fact they brought their problems with them. Saint Benedict called them 'gyrovagues'.[43]

The early Irish monks do not seem to have placed great emphasis on stability. In contrast, one of the ideas they valued was *peregrinatio* – being in foreign parts or travelling around. (This concept will be explored more fully in the next chapter.) In the thirteenth century the mendicant orders, popularly called the Orders of Friars, came to Ireland: namely the Dominicans, Franciscans, Augustinian Friars and Carmelites. Practising itinerancy as part of the apostolic life, their travelling around had the purpose of preaching the Gospel. The mendicant movement was something new in the Church, but was also a continuation of the tradition of Augustinian-type monasticism. The Carmelites began in the desert tradition, but when they took on the mendicant way of life, they combined the two monastic traditions.[44]

When the mendicants came to Ireland, their spirituality fitted in very well with what had been inherited from the pre-twelfth-century Church. There were many points of affinity between them and the early Irish monks. In Ireland the mendicants were able to bridge the gap between what had been a very rural Church and the new situation of people living in towns. The friars were very effective as preachers and confessors, while also providing a ministry to marginalised groups like lepers. It was the friars who carried on the tradition of learning and scholarship which had been such a feature of early Irish monasticism.

Saint Dominic founded his order specifically as an order of preachers. He started his religious life as an Augustinian canon very like those admired by St Malachy, and retained the Rule of St Augustine for his new order. The Dominicans arrived in Ireland in 1224. Although their early foundations were in the Anglo-Norman towns, Gaelic Ireland quickly welcomed them and there were many foundations all over Ireland.

Some of the early Irish saints like St Kevin and St Ciarán are often compared to St Francis of Assisi, because of their love of nature and animals. So it is not surprising that the

Franciscan Order grew rapidly once it came to Ireland. Although the apostolate of the friars was mainly in the towns, some of the Franciscan houses were in remote parts of the country in places of great natural beauty conducive to contemplation, like Timoleague in west Cork. As well as the friars and nuns who formed the First and Second Orders respectively, St Francis also founded a Third Order specifically for lay people who wanted to live the Franciscan spirituality. The secular tertiaries (members of the Third Order), although involved in normal secular activities and occupations, lived according to a demanding rule of life. For instance, they were not allowed to bear arms. There were groups of tertiaries wherever there were friaries. There were also many communities of tertiaries in rural areas in Ireland. Colmán Ó Clabaigh writes:

> The secular tertiaries gave expression in Gaelic Ireland to that burgeoning lay piety that was such a feature of the period throughout Europe. In a predominantly rural society, they provided a spiritual and devotional focus that in more urbanised areas gave rise to guilds and devotional confraternities.[45]

These communities have features in common with the Order of Penitents in the early Church, such as ascetical practices like fasting. They also have a parallel in the early Irish monasteries where the laity, who formed the wider community of the monastery, were all regarded as *manaigh* and lived according to a monastic regime to some extent. The Franciscans fitted into the Irish scene very well and came to see themselves as the preservers of the Irish tradition.

The Augustinian Friars or Eremites of St Augustine also came to Ireland in the thirteenth century. This order was distinct from the canons regular, but also based its spirituality on the Rule of St Augustine. It began with the coming together of groups of hermits in Italy and adopted the mendicant way of life. Some of the branches of this order ran hospitals and hospices for lepers.

The Carmelites began as hermits in the Holy Land. Then they received a community rule from St Albert of Jerusalem. Before becoming Patriarch of Jerusalem, St Albert had been Bishop of Bobbio for twenty years and had started out as a canon regular of Mortura,[46] so he would have been familiar with the Rules of Augustine, Benedict and Columbanus. Saint Albert refers to the earlier Rules in his Introduction:

> Many and varied are the ways in which our saintly forefathers laid down how everyone, whatever his station or the kind of religious life he has chosen, should live a life of allegiance to Jesus Christ.[47]

Saint Albert's Rule is shorter than the earlier ones, yet it contains all the essentials. It is a distillation of the accumulated wisdom of the monastic tradition. His emphasis on solitary meditation in one's cell (Chapter Seven) shows the influence of both the desert and of early Irish monasticism, while his final advice on discretion or common sense shows the influence of St Benedict (Chapter Eighteen). The Rule of Carmel describes the monastic settlement as a collection of individual cells surrounding a chapel (Chapters Three and

Ten). This could be a description of an Irish monastery like Gougane Barra in Cork. So in many ways the Carmelites are very close to early Irish monasticism which also had its roots in the Middle East. When the Carmelites found it necessary to leave the Holy Land and come to Europe, they took on the way of life of the mendicants. This evolution from hermits, to community, to mission is similar to what happened in many of the early Irish monasteries.

The Dissolution of the Monasteries

A serious threat to the continuity of religious life came in the sixteenth century when King Henry VIII ordered the dissolution of the monasteries. The first religious house to be suppressed in Ireland was the Augustinian monastery of All Hallows in Dublin, which was dissolved and its property confiscated by the Crown in 1538. I have given an account in the Appendix of the impact of the dissolution on the principal religious houses in the Diocese of Waterford and Lismore, which may be taken as an example of how it played out. Most of the monasteries had been suppressed by 1541. The pattern of suppression of religious houses in Waterford and Lismore was typical for the eastern part of Ireland which was under the control of the king of England. Further west, things moved more slowly and many monasteries managed to keep going in a precarious existence for another century. Oliver Cromwell's campaign in Ireland, 1649–50, completed the process begun by the dissolution. Michael Olden says that '[the decade] 1650–60 was probably the most difficult and cruel decade that the Irish Catholic Church has ever endured.'[48]

In summary, we can say that the Benedictines, Cistercians and canons regular died out, but the friars managed to survive, despite the loss of their monasteries. Autonomy and stability worked against the older monastic orders. With no actual monasteries in Ireland they could not get any postulants. Anyone wanting to join these orders had to enter monasteries on the continent. This would eventually lead to the return of the Cistercians to Ireland with the founding of Mount Melleray, County Waterford, in 1832. The Benedictines returned to Ireland in 1927 at Glenstal, County Limerick.

Survival and Continuity

The mendicant orders managed to survive the dissolution of the monasteries for a number of reasons: they were not as dependent on having an actual monastery; their establishments were more modest and their communities smaller; mobility was part of their spirituality and this enabled them to move around the country to find safe places of hiding; their closeness to the people meant that there were always people ready to help them. The fact that each community was part of a province was also crucial. People could be drafted in from another house when the need arose. The seminaries on the continent also played a vital role during this period, both for the religious and for the diocesan clergy. The Irish Franciscans had colleges in a number of centres. Their foundations in Louvain (1606), Rome (1625) and Prague (1631) were of great significance for the Catholic Church in Ireland.[49] The Irish Dominicans had colleges in Louvain, Lisbon and Rome. The Augustinians also had a college in Rome, while there were colleges for the secular clergy in many European cities such as Rome, Lisbon, Salamanca, Toulouse and Paris.[50]

Irish Franciscan Scholars

It was the Franciscans above all who carried on the tradition of learning, which had been such a remarkable feature of early Irish monasticism. The friars in Louvain set themselves the task of conserving Irish culture. In the process they compiled a great collection of Irish manuscripts. *The Annals of the Four Masters* were completed by Michael O'Cleary, Fearfeasa Ó Maolconaire, Cúcoigcríche Ó Duibhgennáin and Cúcoigcríche O'Cleary in 1637. The first book in Irish to be printed using a Gaelic font was a catechism written by Fr Bonaventure O'Hussey, titled *Teagasc Críosdaidhe.* It was printed in Antwerp in 1611 and later reprinted in Louvain and in Rome. The Louvain friars also produced a number of other devotional works in Irish, such as *Scáthán Shacramuinte na hAthridhe* by Aodh MacAingil.[51]

Luke Wadding, Irish Franciscan Friar and historian, was born in Waterford in 1588, the eleventh of fourteen children in a very pious family. Both parents died when Luke was fourteen, and his education was then taken in hand by his older brother, Matthew. The Waddings were merchants, engaged in trade with the continent, and so when Matthew went to Portugal on business the following year, he brought Luke with him. While they were there Luke was accepted as a student by the Irish College in Lisbon, which had been founded ten years earlier by a Wexford Jesuit. The following year, 1604, Luke entered the Franciscan Order along with another Irish student, Richard Synott. After completing a course in philosophy, they studied theology in Lisbon and then in Coimbra, where one of their professors was the famous Jesuit, Francisco Suárez.[52]

After his ordination to the priesthood in 1613, Luke's theological ability came to the notice of the Vicar General of the Franciscans who arranged for him to continue his studies in Salamanca. From there Luke went on to Alba de Tormes to study Hebrew and later returned to Salamanca to teach theology in the university. It was through his Spanish connections that he came to Rome in 1618 at the age of thirty. He was to live in that city for the rest of his life and play a huge role in the fortunes of the Irish Church through his influence there. He came to Rome as theological advisor to Bishop Antonio de Trejo, who had been sent there as an extraordinary ambassador of King Philip III of Spain, to petition Pope Paul V to define the doctrine of the Immaculate Conception.[53]

Father Luke Wadding was very good at what is now called networking. He had contacts with members of the papal court and the Roman nobility. The beautiful church and friary of St Isidore's had been built for a group of Spanish Franciscans, but they ran into debt. With the help of his friends, Wadding was able to clear the debt and acquired St Isidore's for the Irish Franciscans. Saint Isidore's College opened in 1625 with Wadding as guardian. A number of the Irish friars in Louvain were transferred there to form the teaching staff.

In the same year that he founded St Isidore's, Luke Wadding also became the co-founder and superior of the Irish College for the diocesan clergy. Cardinal Ludovico Ludovisi had been appointed Cardinal Protector of Ireland by Pope Urban VIII and was looking for practical ways in which he could help the Irish Church. A seminary to train Irish priests was a worthwhile project and Ludovisi turned to Wadding for help. The Irish College was originally located across the street from St Isidore's and shared its staff. In 1639 it moved to Via degli Ibernesi and was run by the Jesuits.[54]

Luke Wadding was a great scholar. He pioneered Franciscan studies, going to Assisi to collect the writings of St Francis and other documents relevant to the history of the Order. He produced an eight-volume history of the Franciscans. He was also the driving force behind the first critical edition of the works of Blessed Duns Scotus on which a number of scholars collaborated. Saint Isidore's became a centre of Scotist studies. The Irish Franciscans were particularly devoted to the teaching of Scotus, because they believed he was Irish. It is now generally accepted that he was Scottish, but the term *Scotus* usually meant Irish in the Middle Ages. As well as this, Scotus was the great exponent of the doctrine of the Immaculate Conception of the Blessed Virgin Mary. It was to promote this doctrine that Luke Wadding had come to Rome in the first place. He wrote three works on Our Lady himself.[55] Luke Wadding died on 18 November 1657.

Among the many other Franciscan scholars of note, three may be mentioned. John Colgan taught Irish History in Louvain. He collected material on the Irish saints and published a number of volumes, including one on the three patrons, St Patrick, St Brigid and St Columba.[56] John Punch was one of the scholars who worked with Wadding to produce the *Opera Omnia* of Scotus. He developed a new method of teaching scholastic philosophy, dividing it into tracts on logic, metaphysics, ethics and so on.

This became the accepted approach in all seminaries.[57] Bonaventure Baron was Wadding's nephew. He travelled all over Europe, going from friary to friary, studying and writing. He published a three-volume work in defence of Scotus (Cologne, 1664) and also wrote treatises on the Immaculate Conception, the Trinity, Angels, Silence and many other topics.[58]

Recovery

As we have seen, the mendicant orders managed to survive the dissolution of the monasteries and the difficult period which followed. They were able to continue their way of life and their ministry in a hidden way in the sixteenth and seventeenth centuries. Paradoxically, the seventeenth century was a golden age of scholarship and learning among the Irish Franciscans on the continent. This was for the purpose of revitalising the Church at home in Ireland.

As the eighteenth century progressed, the friars – like the secular clergy – were able to carry on their ministry more and more openly. The nineteenth century was a period of reconstruction and expansion for all sectors of the Catholic Church in Ireland. Friaries and churches were built, many of them close to or actually on the former medieval sites. I have given a detailed account in the Appendix of the recovery of the friars in the Diocese of Waterford and Lismore. The pattern was much the same throughout the country.

Conclusion

The story of religious life in Ireland is one of remarkable continuity. It has taken many different forms over the centuries, but the core values of religious life have been preserved. Although the particular forms of religious life found in Ireland before the twelfth century have not survived, I think we can be justified in saying that the religious communities which we have today, especially those of a more monastic type of lifestyle, are the successors of early Irish monasticism.

The secular clergy in Ireland can also be seen, in some way, as the successors of the early Irish monks. Originally monks and abbots were not priests, but in Ireland the abbot was usually a priest. All the famous Irish abbots like St Finnian, St Colmcille and St Columbanus were priests. The practice of ordaining priests within the monastery to say private Masses became a growing trend from the seventh century onwards. This trend may have been influenced by Irish monasteries founded on the continent by St Columbanus and others. Ireland was by no means isolated from the rest of the Church. There was influence in both directions. Eoin de Bhaldraithe, in his commentary on the Rule of Carthage, points out that the early Irish abbot was in effect a parish priest, because he was in charge of a church and had pastoral care of the laity in the district as well as of the monks.[59] The Irish parish priest of the nineteenth and early twentieth centuries had something of the early Irish abbot about him. He was not usually a timid character.

Many aspects of the spirituality of early Irish monasticism are still with us: the intense spirit of prayer is still to be found in most religious communities and parishes and in many homes; the emphasis on penance and asceticism may be seen in places like Lough Derg and in Cistercian monasteries;

the high regard for learning for which the early monasteries were noted is still very much part of Irish culture. In Ireland in the past two centuries all the religious orders and all the dioceses had educational institutions to continue the work of education. There were also congregations founded in Ireland specifically to further the work of education. This movement began with Nano Nagle. The missionary spirit of early Irish Christianity continued down through the centuries and saw a great expansion in the nineteenth and twentieth centuries. This missionary spirit is still alive. Another area of Irish spirituality that is alive and well is that of pilgrimage. We will have a look at both mission and pilgrimage in the next chapter.

NOTES

1. I have taken the dates for figures in early Christianity from Joseph F. Kelly, *The Concise Dictionary of Early Christianity* (Collegeville: The Liturgical Press, 1992).
2. *The Sayings of the Desert Fathers*, revised edition, Benedicta Ward SLG, trans. (Oxford: Mowbray, 1981), p. 9.
3. Cf. John R. Walsh and Thomas Bradley, *A History of the Irish Church 400–700 AD* (Dublin: Columba Press, 2003), p. 32.
4. Rule of St Augustine, ch. 1, 2; Cf. *The Rule of St Augustine with Introduction & Commentary*, Raymond Canning OSA, trans. (London: Darton, Longman & Todd, 1984).
5. Acts 4:32-35.
6. Cf. 1 Corinthians 8: 32-38.
7. St Hippolytus, *The Apostolic Tradition*, 12.
8. Rule of St Augustine, ch. 7, 3.
9. Canning, op. cit., p. 81.
10. St Patrick, *Confessio*, 41.
11. Cf. T. M. Charles-Edwards, *Early Christian Ireland* (Cambridge: Cambridge University Press, 2000), pp. 223–6.

12. Michael Richter suggests that this is where the concept comes from. Cf. Michael Richter, *Medieval Ireland: The Enduring Tradition* (Dublin: Gill and Macmillan, 1988), p. 62.
13. Cf. T. M. Charles-Edwards, *Early Christian Ireland*, pp. 244–51.
14. Brian Lacey, *Saint Columba His Life and Legacy* (Dublin: Columba Press, 2013), pp. 146–8.
15. Brian Lacey, *Saint Columba His Life and Legacy*, pp. 192–4.
16. Peter O'Dwyer OCarm, *Towards a History of Irish Spirituality* (Dublin: Columba Press, 1995), pp. 43–6.
17. O'Dwyer, op. cit., pp. 53–7.
18. The Rule of Carthage in Uinseann Ó Maidín OCR, *The Celtic Monk Rules & Writings of Early Irish Monks* (Kalamazoo: Cistercian Publications, 1996), pp. 67–70.
19. Cf. Tomás Cardinal Ó Fiaich, 'The Beginnings of Christianity 5th and 6th Centuries', *The Course of Irish History*, revised edition, T. W. Moody and F. X. Martin, eds (Dublin: Mercier Press, 2001).
20. Cf. T. M. Charles-Edwards, *Early Christian Ireland*, ch. 6.
21. The Faddan More Psalter was discovered in a bog in north Tipperary in 2006. The Book of Psalms is divided into three groups of fifty psalms corresponding to the usage of the Céli Dé. Cf. Karen O'Donovan, 'The Faddan More Psalter', *New Liturgy*, No. 150 (Summer 2011), pp 14–16.
22. Bede, *A History of the English Church and People* Leo Sherley-Price, trans. (Harmondsworth, Middlesex: Penguin Books, 1968), Book 3, ch. 27, p. 195.
23. Cf. Tomás Ó Fiaich, *Columbanus in His Own Words* (Dublin: Veritas, 1990), p. 22.
24. Cf. Dáibhí Ó Crónáin, 'A Tale of Two Rules: Benedict and Columbanus', *The Irish Benedictines: A History*, Martin Browne OSB and Colmán Ó Clabaigh OSB (Dublin: Columba Press, 2005), pp. 15–17.
25. This was contrary to Columbanus's wishes. Cf. Ó Fiaich, op. cit., pp. 47–5.
26. St Columbanus, Letter to Pope Boniface IV, translated by Tomás Ó Fiaich, op. cit., p. 81.
27. St Columbanus, Letter to a Young Disciple, translated by Tomás Ó Fiaich, op. cit., p. 85.
28. Cf. Ó Fiaich, op. cit., p. 48.

29. There is a fine translation of this letter *Celtic Spirituality,* Oliver Davies, ed. (New York: Paulist Press, 1999), pp. 359–62.
30. Cf. Frank Lawrence, 'What did they sing at Cashel in 1172? Winchester, Sarum and Romano-Frankish Chant in Ireland', *The Journal of the Society for Musicology in Ireland*, vol. 3 (2007–8), pp. 121–4.
31. Cf. R. W. Southern, *Western Society and the Church in the Middle Ages* (Harmondsworth: Penguin Books, 1970), pp. 241–3.
32. Cf. John Watt, *The Church in Medieval Ireland* (Dublin: Gill and Macmillan, 1972), p. 16.
33. Cf. Watt, op. cit., p. 45.
34. Brian Lacey, O'Brien, *Pocket History of Irish Saints* (Dublin: O'Brien Press, 2003), p. 116.
35. Cf. Watt, op. cit., pp. 44–5.
36. Watt, op. cit., pp 16–17.
37. Cf. Marie Therese Flanagan, *The Transformation of the Irish Church in the Twelfth Century* (Woodbridge: The Boydell Press, 2010), p. 134.
38. Cf. Brian Lacey, O'Brien, *Pocket History of Irish Saints*, pp. 118–22.
39. Ruth Dudley Edwards, *An Atlas of Irish History*, second edition, (London, 1981), p. 124.
40. John Ryan, 'The Mass in the Early Irish Church', *Studies*, vol. 50 (1961), p. 375.
41. Cf. Brian Lacey, *Saint Columba His Life and Legacy*, pp. 192–4.
42. Aubrey Gwynn SJ, 'The Antiphonary of Armagh', *The Journal of the County Louth Archaeological Society*, vol. 11 (1945), pp. 5–6.
43. Rule of St Benedict, ch. 1. Cf. *St. Benedict's Rule for Monasteries* Leonard J. Doyle, trans. (Collegeville: The Liturgical Press, 1948).
44. Although they began as hermits in a secluded location, the Carmelites did not, at any stage, have an abbot, which was one of the defining characteristics of desert monasticism. They sought a rule from the bishop which points to the Augustinian type and, in fact, St Albert, who wrote the Rule was an Augustinian.
45. Colmán Ó Clabaigh OSB, *The Friars in Ireland 1224–1540* (Dublin: Four Courts Press, 2012), pp. 316–17.
46. Cf. Wilfrid McGreal OCarm, *At the Fountain of Elijah: The Carmelite Tradition* (London, 1999), pp. 19–20.

47. The Rule of Carmel, Introduction. The full text of the rule is to be found in McGreal, op. cit., pp. 21–6.
48. Olden, *The Life and Times of Patrick Comerford OSA (1586–1652) Counter-Reformation Bishop of Waterford and Lismore 1629–1652* (Waterford, 2012), p. 182.
49. Cf. Patrick Conlan OFM, *Franciscan Ireland* (Dublin: Mercier, 1978), p. 31.
50. Cf. Edwards, op. cit., pp 142-43.
51. Cf. Patrick Conlan OFM, *Franciscan Ireland*, p. 37.
52. Cf. Patrick Conlan OFM, *St Isidore's College Rome* (Rome, 1982), pp. 31–5.
53. Cf. Conlan, *St Isidore's*, pp. 36–7. The dogma of the Immaculate Conception of Our Lady was defined by Blessed Pius IX in 1854.
54. Cf. John J. Hanley, *The Irish College*, Rome, Irish Heritage Series no. 64, (Norwich: Eason and Son, 1989), pp. 1–3.
55. Cf. Conlan, *St Isidore's*, p. 73.
56. Ibid., pp. 77–9.
57. Ibid., pp. 79–80.
58. Ibid., pp. 80–2.
59. Cf. Eoin de Bhaldraithe, 'The Rule of Carthage', *Hallel* (Winter 1987), p. 205.

CHAPTER TWO

PILGRIMAGE, EXILE AND MISSION: THE SPIRITUALITY OF BEING AWAY FROM HOME

Pilgrimage, exile and mission may all be included under the general heading of *peregrinatio*, which basically means being in foreign parts or travelling around. What all of these situations have in common is the experience of displacement. One is deprived of one's usual surroundings and the supports upon which one normally relies. This makes one more aware of the need to trust in God's providence.

There are many examples of *peregrinatio* in the Bible. The story of the Chosen People begins with the call of Abraham. 'Go from your country and your kindred and your father's house to the land that I will show you' (Gn 12:1). When Abraham responded to this call, he went out into the unknown. He did not know where it would lead and his response was an act of faith, wherein he became a pilgrim, relying on God to guide and protect him. His descendants would have to hold the same trust in God. They would be a pilgrim people. The call of Abraham became a paradigm for the early Irish *peregrini*. The quoted text was favoured and frequently applied to those who went abroad to be pilgrims for Christ. Jonas, in his *Life of St Columban*, says that after he had been many years in the cloister, Columbanus longed to go to foreign lands in obedience to the command that the Lord had given to Abraham.[1]

The medieval *Life of Colum Cille* provides a theology of *peregrinatio*.[2] The author says that all the faithful are called, like Abraham, to leave all things for the sake of the Lord of Creation and to go on pilgrimage. There are three ways in which a person goes on pilgrimage. The first is to leave home in body only, without leaving behind one's vices and attachments. This kind of pilgrimage is of no value whatsoever. The second is where a person remains at home physically, because the duties of their state of life require it, as in the case of priests, but go on pilgrimage spiritually. This means to leave home in desire of heart. The Lord accepts this as a pilgrimage.

The third kind of pilgrimage is what the author calls the perfect pilgrimage, where a person leaves home completely in body and soul. Those who undertake this are like the twelve apostles to whom the Lord promised the hundredfold reward for leaving everything to follow him. So it would seem that in the Irish tradition pilgrimage is essentially about detachment. If one has this attitude, one can be a pilgrim without actually going anywhere. However, the physical pilgrimage helps to express and cultivate this attitude. Pilgrimage is undertaken for the love of God and in order to follow Christ like the twelve apostles. This suggests an openness to mission.

If Abraham was the archetypal pilgrim, his grandson Jacob was a person who experienced a series of displacements over the course of his life. Jacob left the home of his parents more out of necessity than in response to any call. His brother Esau had threatened to kill him for having tricked their father into giving him the blessing of the firstborn, and so his mother sent him off to her brother to be out of harm's way. This, however, involved a journey of a few hundred miles on foot and alone. So it is not surprising if he felt pretty wretched when he stopped for the night. It was then that God was revealed to him as his protector and friend, through a dream in which Jacob saw angels going up and down a ladder to heaven.[3] Jacob continued on his journey and was welcomed by his uncle's family.

Jacob spent fourteen years working for his uncle Laban in Haran. During this time he married both Leah and Rachel and became a wealthy man with flocks of sheep and goats and herds of cattle and camels. Eventually, he wanted to return to the land of Canaan. On the way he had another life-changing experience, like the one he had had on the outward journey. Like the dream of the ladder, this second experience also related to his fear of his brother Esau.

Esau had also acquired a large following in the intervening years. As he journeyed along, Jacob received a message that Esau was coming to meet him. He was afraid that Esau still intended to kill him. He sent his family across the ford of the Jabbok and spent a very restless night on his own. A mysterious being came and wrestled with him all night. As day was breaking, Jacob held on to the wrestler until he received a blessing. The blessing was that Jacob received a new name, Israel, which means 'strength of God'. The being also dislocated Jacob's hip and refused to reveal his own name. Jacob realised that he had been struggling with God. At the conclusion of the encounter, Jacob says: 'I have seen God face to face, and yet my life is preserved' (Gn 32:30). He called the place Peniel, meaning 'face of God'.

This incident has been interpreted as meaning that we have to struggle with God in prayer. One way of looking at it is to say that we are lucky if we lose the struggle, because then we rely on God's strength. Jacob limped away from Peniel, but now he was not relying on his own cunning, but on God's strength. The real significance of the incident is shown in what happens next. Jacob goes on to meet his brother with some trepidation. Esau had threatened to kill him the last time they met, but Esau receives him graciously. Jacob's reaction is to say: 'truly to see your face is like seeing the face of God' (Gn 33:10). Jacob has gained new insight from his encounter with God. Now he is able to recognise God's presence in his brother.

After many years of being settled in the land of Canaan, Israel was again uprooted. His son Joseph had been sold as a slave by his brothers. He had ended up in Egypt, where his gift of interpreting dreams had not only got him released from slavery and imprisonment, but had made him chief advisor to Pharaoh, the King of Egypt. When famine came to the region, Joseph had prudently prepared for the crisis by stockpiling grain. His brothers came to Egypt in order to buy grain. Joseph arranged for the whole family to move to Egypt. He died in exile in Egypt, but his body was brought back to the land of Canaan to be buried in the cave that Abraham had bought as a burial place when his wife Sarah died.[4]

Further on in the story of the Chosen People we find the Israelites wandering in the desert for forty years. Before entering the Promised Land, Moses invites them to look back and reflect on their experience.

> Remember the long way that the Lord your God has led you these forty years in the wilderness, in

> order to humble you, testing you to know what was in your heart, whether or not you would keep his commandments. He humbled you by letting you hunger, then by feeding you with manna, with which neither you nor your ancestors were acquainted, in order to make you understand that one does not live by bread alone, but by every word that comes from the mouth of the Lord. The clothes on your back did not wear out and your feet did not swell all those forty years. (Deut 8:2-4)

It was not so much God who needed to know what was in the hearts of the Israelites. God already knows what is in people's hearts. It was they themselves who needed to get in touch with their deepest desires and to be clear in their minds about their commitment to their covenant with the Lord. Moses points out to the people that though they experienced hardship, their essential needs were looked after by divine providence. Most importantly, they became aware of the deeper spiritual need that can only be satisfied by God. Human beings do not live on bread alone, but on the Word of God. The above passage from Deuteronomy expresses well the pilgrimage experience. If undertaken in the right spirit, it leads to greater self-knowledge and humility. It also involves getting in touch with our deeper spiritual desires and relying on divine providence.

The pilgrimage of the Magi in St Matthew's Gospel (cf. Mt 2:1-12) is a physical journey, a spiritual journey and a parable for our lives. They are a mysterious group. The Gospel calls them *magoi*, meaning wise men or astrologers. The most significant thing about them is that they are complete outsiders, coming from the exotic 'East'. They do not belong to the Jewish faith, but have their own religious beliefs. They remind us that all religions are searching for God, searching for the truth.

The Magi follow the star. They follow the light that has been given to them. Sometimes they can see it; at other times it disappears, but they keep journeying on. When they cannot find their way they consult the experts. Their lives are changed by the encounter with Jesus. They went back to their own country by a different way. This may be taken to mean not just that they avoided Herod, but that they lived in a different way.

The Finding in the Temple (cf. Lk 2:41-50) is the story of the Holy Family on pilgrimage. Saint Luke tells us that every year the parents of Jesus went to Jerusalem for the feast of the Passover.[5] However, this may have been the first time that they brought Jesus along with them. At twelve years old he would have celebrated his *Bar Mitzvah*. Indeed, this ceremony may well have taken place in Jerusalem during the pilgrimage. The *Bar Mitzvah* meant taking on the obligations of the covenant and so taking a full part in the religious life of the Jewish people. For a young boy from a small town in the north of Israel, visiting a great city and religious centre like Jerusalem for the first time would have been a great experience. So it is not surprising that Jesus wanted to explore and that he was particularly fascinated by the temple. Saint Luke probably wants to underline the three days Jesus' parents spent looking for him in order to point to the three days of his death and resurrection which also took place in Jerusalem. It is not as extraordinary as may first appear. The first day was spent on the journey home without realising Jesus was not with the group of pilgrims from Nazareth. It would have taken another day to get back to Jerusalem and they found him on the third day.

What is most significant is what Mary says when Jesus is found: 'My son, why have you done this to us. See how worried your father and I have been, looking for you.' Like any parent, Mary was worried. She did not say: 'He is the Son of God. Nothing can happen to him.' No angel appeared to tell her he was safe. So Mary had to live by faith. Like the rest of us, she did not always understand what was happening or how God's plan was unfolding. Knowing who Jesus was did not spare her from suffering.

As an adult Jesus goes up to Jerusalem for the pilgrimage festivals. Saint John's Gospel pays particular attention to this. The pilgrimage to Jerusalem for the Feast of Tabernacles is particularly interesting. The feast was a harvest festival, which also commemorated the forty years that the people of Israel spent wandering in the desert. It took its name from the booths or tents constructed to symbolise this period. A particularly joyful festival, it went on for a week,[6] with rituals including an elaborate procession with containers of water brought to the temple to be poured over the altar and also an illumination of the temple area at night with four great candelabras. As the temple was on top of a hill, this must have been a great sight visible from all over the city and particularly striking from the Mount of Olives.

The account in John begins with a discussion among Jesus' relatives as to whether or not Jesus will go to the festival. This suggests that his normal practice would have been to attend, but on this occasion there is a threat to his life. Jesus let the group of pilgrims from Nazareth head off without him, but went to the festival later without drawing attention to himself. About halfway through the week he went to the temple and began to teach.[7] On the last day of the festival Jesus applied the two great symbols of water and light to himself:

> Let anyone who is thirsty come to me, and let the one who believes in me drink. As the scripture has said, 'out of the believer's heart shall flow rivers of living water'. (Jn 7:37-38)
>
> I am the light of the world. Whoever follows me will never walk in darkness but will have the light of life. (Jn 8:12)

Jerusalem is the Holy City of the Jews. For Christians it has the further significance of being the place where many of the important events in Jesus' life took place. Jerusalem was where Jesus spent the last weeks of his life, where he instituted the Eucharist and where he died and rose again. Jerusalem has continued to be the place of pilgrimage *par excellence.* Interest in the holy places developed considerably after the Peace of Constantine in AD 313. Constantine's mother, St Helen, went to the Holy Land to find relics of the True Cross and had churches built to commemorate the events in the life of Jesus. Jerusalem has continued to attract pilgrims down through the ages. One such pilgrim was St Ignatius of Loyola.

Saint Ignatius the Pilgrim

Saint Ignatius of Loyola in his *Autobiography*, written in the third person, refers to himself for most of the narrative as 'the pilgrim'. He also gives an account of his pilgrimage to the Holy Land. It is a most interesting story. Up to the age of twenty-six Ignatius had been pursuing his career as a soldier, but having been wounded in battle, he spent some time convalescing in the home of his brother. During this time he experienced a spiritual awakening. He became aware of the various thoughts and images going through his imagination. He found that when he dwelt on worldly pursuits, they gave him pleasure at the time, but afterwards left him feeling dejected. On the other hand, when he thought about spiritual things, like the heroic deeds of the saints, he felt encouraged and consoled and this feeling remained with him. One of these spiritual thoughts was the idea of going barefoot to Jerusalem. So he resolved that he would go to Jerusalem as soon as he recovered from his injuries.[8]

As things turned out, it was about a year after his recovery that he set out on his pilgrimage, in the spring of 1523. Getting from Spain to the Holy Land in those days was no easy matter. Ignatius wanted to rely completely on God, so he decided to go alone and to beg his way. He got sick a number of times and had to depend on the good will of strangers for assistance. He went by ship from Barcelona to Italy, disembarking at Gaeta and walking to Rome. From there he had to get to Venice and take another sea voyage to Cypress and then on to another ship, which was carrying a group of pilgrims to the port of Jaffa. Here the pilgrims were supplied with donkeys for the journey to Jerusalem.[9]

Ignatius says that when they came in sight of the Holy City they were filled with a joy that was more than natural. He felt the same devotion when he visited the various holy sites in Jerusalem. It is known from the diary of another pilgrim that these included Mount Sion, the Cenacle, the Church of the Dormition of Mary, the Holy Sepulchre and Gethsemane. They also walked the Way of the Cross and visited Bethlehem and Jericho.[10] Ignatius himself mentions visiting Mount Olivet where Our Lord ascended into heaven. He went back a second time to get an exact picture of it in his mind. So it would seem that he wanted to picture the life of Christ in his imagination, in order to meditate on it. This is something he proposed later when he wrote the *Spiritual Exercises*. He wanted to stay in Jerusalem so that he could continually visit the scenes of Christ's earthly life. However, the Franciscans, who were the custodians of the holy places, advised against it, and when he pressed his case the provincial threatened him with excommunication if he did not leave. This was for his own safety as many Europeans had been kidnapped and held to ransom. Ignatius accepted this as the will of God and decided to go back to Spain.[11]

The return journey was even more adventurous than the outward one. This was in the middle of winter, with freezing temperatures and stormy seas. On his way from Venice to Genoa, Ignatius got caught up in a war which was going on between France and the Holy Roman Empire. He was captured twice, first by the Imperial troops who thought he was a spy and the second time by the French, because he was in the wrong place at the wrong time. The Imperial captain released him, because he thought he was insane, while the French captain treated him to a meal when he discovered that Ignatius was a fellow Basque.[12]

The pilgrimage to Jerusalem was very fruitful for Ignatius. He went there with the intention of spending his life in contemplation. While there he discovered that his vocation would involve sharing the fruits of contemplation with others. Had the Franciscans agreed to his request to become a hermit in Jerusalem, the Jesuits would never have been founded. When Ignatius realised that it was not God's will that he should stay in Jerusalem, he decided to go back to school so that he could study in order to equip himself to help souls.[13] The future was not clear to Ignatius as he returned to Spain, but he had a new direction and a new purpose.

Other Places of Pilgrimage

Saint Cathal was an Irish pilgrim to the Holy Land in the seventh century. On his return journey he was shipwrecked off the southern coast of Italy and came ashore at Taranto, where he was prevailed upon by the local people to stay. He went on to become Archbishop of Taranto.[14] Rome was a more popular destination for Irish pilgrims. The early Irish had a great devotion to the See of Peter. Not having been subjects of the Roman Empire, they were able to see Rome purely as a spiritual centre. Another important centre of pilgrimage in medieval times was Compostela, which holds the shrine of St James.

A pilgrimage often takes the form of a journey to a particular holy place in order to pray or do penance. Before the advent of modern transport, taking on such a journey was a penance in itself because of the hardship and hazards involved. In recent years there has been a revival of interest in pilgrim routes and the experience of walking. This is especially the case with the pilgrimage to the shrine of the apostle St James at Compostela, known as the Camino. The journey is at least as important as the destination.

Apart from the inherent penitential aspect involved in getting to the holy place, two of the earliest Irish pilgrimages were decidedly penitential in themselves. These are Croagh Patrick and Lough Derg, both places associated with St Patrick. Croagh Patrick is Ireland's holy mountain. It was probably a place of pilgrimage in pre-Christian times. Traditionally, St Patrick is believed to have spent forty days and nights on the mountain, fasting and praying like Moses on Mount Sinai. Many thousands of pilgrims climb the Reek every year, especially on Reek Sunday which is the last Sunday in July. There is a small chapel on the summit where Mass is celebrated on that day. Pilgrims can begin the climb at the foot of the mountain, or if they want to do a longer walk, they can start at Ballintubber Abbey and walk the traditional Tóchar Phádraig. There is a great sense of solidarity among pilgrims and the views are stunning.[15]

Lough Derg is a small lake in the south-east corner of County Donegal. In the lake, there is a small island called Station Island or St Patrick's Purgatory. Here pilgrims come to fast and pray. The traditional pilgrimage involves spending three days and two nights on the island. One of the nights is spent in vigil. Pilgrims say set numbers of Our Fathers and Hail Marys while going around little rocky areas with crosses, known as 'beds' in their bare feet. It is a very intense experience and has always attracted pilgrims from near and far. During the Middle Ages there was a cave on the island where pilgrims spent a night and some were said to have had visions of Purgatory. Now there is a fine basilica where Mass is celebrated. The Sacrament of Reconciliation is also an important part of this pilgrimage.[16]

Many of the places of pilgrimage in Ireland are associated with a local saint and have a holy well. Some of the holy wells may have been pre-Christian places of worship. The association of the holy wells with the saints, however, comes from their use as baptisteries. In many places in early Christianity, flowing water was preferred for Baptism.[17] It symbolised better than still water the living water of which Jesus speaks to the Samaritan woman.[18] The practice of drinking the water from the holy well may also be based on this promise of Jesus to give living water to those who believe in him.[19] Holy wells are to be found all over Ireland. Examples are those at Ardmore, Ballyvourney and Clonmacnoise. These are associated with St Declan, St Gobnait and St Ciarán respectively.

Marian Pilgrimages

Marian pilgrimages have a particular significance. Mary herself was a pilgrim, as we have seen in the incident of the Finding in the Temple. The Marian shrines are places of hospitality over which Mary the homemaker presides. They have a particular atmosphere of warmth and peace.

The oldest centre of Marian pilgrimage in Ireland is Our Lady's Island in the south-east corner of Ireland in County Wexford. An island on a lake – or rather more accurately a peninsula, as it is not completely surrounded by water and is accessible by land – according to local tradition it was founded by St Abban and had become established as a place of pilgrimage and of devotion to Our Lady by the end of the sixth century. With the Norman invasion it became part of the estate of the De Lamporte family. In the early thirteenth century Rudolph de Lamporte invited the canons regular of St Augustine to take charge of the island, before he himself left for the Holy Land to die there as a crusader. Our Lady's Island became an important centre of pilgrimage in the Middle Ages. It attracted papal approval in the form of indulgences granted to pilgrims by Pope Martin V (1417–31), while it was also added to a list of approved places of devotion in a letter of encouragement sent to the people of Ireland by Pope Paul V in 1607. Perhaps the most significant piece of official recognition was that given by Pope Benedict XIV in the eighteenth century when he banned all local Irish pilgrimages because of the abuses attached to them, with the exception of Our Lady's Island and Lough Derg. Our Lady's Island continues to attract large numbers of pilgrims every year, both as private individuals and as members of organised pilgrimages. The traditional pilgrimage consists of a visit to the parish church which overlooks the island and lake, followed by a walk around the island reciting fifteen decades of the Rosary and concluding with another visit to the church.[20]

The traditional devotions at holy wells and pilgrimage sites usually involve the recitation of the Rosary or of a certain number of Our Fathers and Hail Marys while 'doing the rounds'. That is, the prayers are recited while walking round the sacred site. This is a very ancient practice. It has the value that it involves the whole person: the mind is occupied with the prayers, while the body is involved in the movement. The other advantage of these traditional devotions is their simplicity. Anyone can do them, individually or in a group, and there is no need for any leader or professional religious person.

Knock in County Mayo became a Marian shrine because of the apparition which took place there on 21 August 1879. The apparition was witnessed by fifteen people and took place at the gable end of the parish church.[21] It lasted a number of hours. The vision took place in silence. Our Lady did not speak, but it would be wrong to conclude from this that there was no message. The apparition itself is so rich in meaning that it becomes clear when we reflect upon it that it has a profound message.

Mary appeared in Knock as Queen and Mother. On her head was a golden crown and she was accompanied by her family. To her left the visionaries identified the figure of St Joseph, the spouse of the Blessed Virgin. To her right they identified St John the Evangelist, traditionally regarded as the beloved disciple who became Mary's son at the foot of the Cross. The statues which are now in the place where the apparition took place beautifully and accurately evoke for us what the visionaries saw. The Blessed Virgin was not at the centre of the apparition. At the centre was Christ himself in the form of the Lamb of God on an altar surrounded by angels. Mary was in an attitude of prayer contemplating Christ present in the Eucharist and at the same time glorified in heaven.[22]

The Lamb of God on the altar is a clear evocation of the Eucharist. The vision at Knock was an encouragement to the Irish people in their devotion to the Mass, to which they had remained faithful through very difficult times. The Eucharist is at the heart of all the Marian shrines. In

Lourdes the Blessed Virgin appeared to Bernadette who was preparing for her first Holy Communion and who had in fact returned to Lourdes because of her desire to do so. Our Lady asked her to tell the priests to have a chapel built for the purpose of the celebration of the Eucharist.

Exile

Exile can be voluntary or involuntary. In many societies banishment was used as a punishment for certain crimes. In Celtic culture, where a person's identity was seen in terms of belonging to a kinship group, to be separated from it was a kind of death. In the case of the early Irish ascetics, exile was usually undertaken as an act of renunciation. One gave up what one loved dearly for the love of God or as a penance for one's sins. Those who undertook the *peregrinatio* in this spirit did so with the intention of not returning.

The people of Israel spent seventy years in exile in Babylon. The exile was a traumatic experience for the Jews. Their first reaction was denial. Before it happened they refused to believe that it really would happen, and then when it did, they said it would not last long. The great prophet of the exile was Jeremiah. Unlike the false prophets who said everything would be all right, Jeremiah predicted the destruction of Jerusalem and the deportation of its population. Once it happened he told them it would last. At the same time his message to the exiles was one of hope:

> For thus says the Lord: Only when Babylon's seventy years are completed will I visit you, and I will fulfil to you my promise and bring you back to this place. For surely I know the plans I have

> for you, says the Lord, plans for your welfare and not for harm, to give you a future with hope. (Jer 29:10-11)

The Lord would give them a new covenant. They would prosper in exile and their descendents would return to the land.

In the experience of exile the people of Israel were deprived of all the familiar supports of their religious life. First of all they lost the land which God had given to their ancestors and from which they derived their identity. Second, they lost the temple which was the focus of their worship of the Lord, the sign of God's presence among them, and their place of pilgrimage for all the great religious festivals. They effectively lost the priesthood, because the priests could not function without the temple. Finally, they lost the monarchy. The monarchy might have been a mixed blessing, but at least they had been governed by one of their own. Now they were ruled by foreigners.

So having been deprived of so much, the Jewish people had to fall back on what they still had. They still had the Word. Once they had come to terms with what had happened, they responded creatively to their new situation. The identity of a people is preserved in its memory and so it became vital to keep the story alive. They became the People of the Book. They met every Sabbath to read the Scriptures and to encourage one another. They continued to observe the moral code given to them in the Ten Commandments and the dietary and other customs which gave them a distinct identity and enabled them to resist being absorbed by the people among whom they lived. They also continued to celebrate the yearly festivals of Passover, Pentecost, the New Year, the Day of Atonement and Tabernacles. They could no longer go to the temple, but they found a way of celebrating these festivals at home. For instance, the Book of Leviticus prescribed elaborate ceremonies for the Day of Atonement.[23] These were to be performed in the temple by the high priest. These ceremonies could no longer be performed, but the people could still observe a day of fasting, prayer and quiet reflection. In this way they preserved the essential meaning of the Day of Atonement. In the crucible of exile the Jews sharpened their identity and refined their religious practice. The synagogue and the scribe came to the fore in the place of the temple and the priest. These remained important after the return from exile and the building of the second temple. More important than either temple or synagogue was the home. It was here that the most important religious rituals were performed and here that the faith was handed on. This remains the great strength of Judaism to this day.

Patrick the Exile

Saint Patrick was an exile twice: the first time involuntarily and the second time by his own choice. The first exile, although a traumatic experience, was to have a positive effect on Patrick's life. In his testament, called the *Confessio*, Patrick tells us that as a youth of sixteen he was like many of his contemporaries and did not know the true God. This statement surprises us, because Patrick also says that his father was a deacon and his grandfather was a priest.[24] So it is likely that he had a Christian upbringing, was taught to pray and took part in the liturgy. So what was missing? It would seem that, as so often happens, religion was part of his upbringing, but it had not become a personal experience for him. It was something outside of himself. To the extent that it was part of his life, it was an outward observance, rather than a life of faith.

All that changed when Patrick was captured by Irish raiders and sold into slavery. Then the seed that had been planted by his parents in his early years began to grow. Just like the seed, which is buried in the ground in autumn, is stimulated by the frosts of winter and comes to life in springtime, so the seed of faith lying dormant in his heart was shocked into life by his traumatic experience and started to grow. Patrick began to pray. He says that he prayed a hundred times in the day and nearly as often in the night. He used to get up before dawn to pray, even in snow or rain, and never felt the worse for it.[25] He began to know God through faith. The experience of faith is often described as obscure, because it cannot be described, measured or explained in the way the experience of the world around us can. God is spirit and is experienced in the depths of our being in a mysterious way.

Being taken captive and sold into slavery meant that Patrick was separated from his family and friends, deprived of an education, taken out of the civilised world that he knew and robbed of his freedom. The shock must have been enormous. Yet, when he looks back on the whole experience as an old man, he sees it as an expression of God's mercy.

> The Lord there made me aware of my unbelief that I might at last advert to my sins and turn wholeheartedly to the Lord my God. He showed

> concern for my weakness, and pity for my youth and ignorance; he watched over me before I got to know him and before I was able to distinguish good from evil. In fact he protected me and comforted me as a father would his son. I cannot be silent then, nor indeed should I, about the great benefits and grace which the Lord saw fit to confer on me in the land of my captivity.[26]

Saint Patrick's second exile was when he came back to Ireland voluntarily as a missionary.

The spiritual descendents of St Patrick would share both of his experiences. This was particularly the case in the wake of the Great Famine of 1845–7. There was a great wave of emigration following the famine. The people who left are regarded as exiles, because their leaving was necessitated by the economic situation. They also left without hope of return.

Mission

One of the interesting aspects of early Irish monasticism, mentioned in the last chapter, was the linking of pilgrimage and mission. Saint Adomnán in his *Life of Columba* tells us that in the forty-second year of his age, Columba sailed away from Ireland to Britain, wishing to be a pilgrim for Christ.[27] This idea of being a pilgrim for Christ seems to have begun with St Columba, or Colum Cille, as he is known in Irish. The idea here was not that of going to a particular place in order to visit it, but to become a permanent pilgrim. To be a pilgrim means not putting down roots, travelling lightly on the earth, being in search of a heavenly homeland (cf.

Heb 11:16). It is, in fact, a particular kind of spirituality. It is interesting that it should have arisen in Ireland, among a people with a strong sense of place.[28] Where Columba went was to Iona, a small, but fertile island in the Inner Hebrides. It appears that the island was given to him by Conall, king of the Scottish part of Dál Riata. The Dál Riata, a Gaelic-speaking people, straddled the North Channel, with one group living in north Antrim and the other in Argyll. That part of Scotland was part of the Gaelic cultural area. Iona was on the northern edge of this territory, so Columba was going to the periphery of the Gaelic world.

There has been much speculation about what motivated this apparently sudden change of course in Columba's life. It has been suggested that exile was imposed upon him as a penance or that he was filled with missionary zeal.[29] It seems to me, however, that Columba was a man who was very open to the inspirations of the Holy Spirit and that he experienced a call. What form this call took we do not know, but as mentioned already, the medieval *Life of Colum Cille* compares it to the call of Abraham. Like Abraham, Columba responded in faith and trusted that the Holy Spirit would show him the next step when the time came.

One thing we can say with reasonable certainty about Columba's intentions when he left Ireland for Iona, was that he intended to found a monastic community. This seems clear from the fact that he brought twelve companions with him in imitation of Christ and the apostles. Since the twelve apostles were a group sent by Christ to preach the Gospel, we can say that Columba and his companions were at least open to the idea of being evangelists and preachers.

In fact, Iona became at least as famous as any monastery in Ireland and played a significant role in the evangelisation of Scotland and northern England.

In the preface to his work, Adomnán tells us that Columba spent thirty-four years as a soldier of Christ on the island of Iona and that all his time was given over to prayer, reading, writing or doing some other good work. His devotion to fasts and vigils was such that it seemed beyond human strength. 'Yet through all he was loving to everyone, his holy face was always cheerful, and in his inmost heart he was happy with the joy of the Holy Spirit.'[30] Adomnán goes on to give anecdotes about the saint's life, arranged thematically in three books under the headings: Prophetic Revelations, Miracles and Angelic Visitations. Even allowing for the exaggerations usual in this type of literature, Columba emerges as a kindly person of deep prayer and spirituality. He was endowed with charismatic gifts by the Holy Spirit, but like many mystics, he could be very practical. As a person coming from a royal background, it was probably inevitable that he would involve himself in the politics of both Ireland and Scotland.

During his time on Iona, St Columba undertook a number of journeys on the Scottish mainland. He travelled up the Great Glen to meet Brude, king of the Northern Picts, at his fortress near Inverness. This led to the conversion of the Picts, among whom the Iona monks worked in the years that followed. Columba is reputed to have encountered the Loch Ness monster on the way, the first mention in literature of that beast so valuable to the tourist industry. Columba's intervention in Scottish politics was decisive. When Conall, king of the Dál Riada Gaels, died, Columba anointed his younger son Aidan to succeed him. The biblical precedent was Samuel anointing David (cf. 1 Sm 16:11-13). That Columba was a true prophet like Samuel was never in doubt. Columba clearly believed that Aidan had been chosen by God. This is the earliest example of the anointing or 'ordination' of a Christian king. A prayer for this purpose in the Leofric Missal is attributed to St Columba. It is remarkable for its emphasis on peace and charity.[31]

Saint Columba also made a number of brief visits to Ireland. The most important one was for the Convention of Druim Ceatt. Here Columba championed the cause of the poets. The High King had wanted to banish them from Ireland, clearly regarding them as a bunch of interfering parasites. The poets were well known to be effective satirists and the only ones who could criticise the powers that be. Columba was a poet himself and he reminded the assembly of how impoverished our culture would be if there were no poets to extol the virtues of brave young men or sing of the beauty of handsome maidens. His arguments won the day. Indeed, by that stage in his life, his prestige and reputation for holiness were such that no one was going to oppose him. He was also successful in gaining an important measure of independence for his adopted country. Henceforth Scottish Dál Riata would not have to pay tribute to the king of Irish Dál Riata.

The name Columba means 'dove' and may have been chosen because the dove is the symbol of the Holy Spirit. Another bird associated with St Columba is the crane. Adomnán tells the story of how one day Columba called one of the monks on Iona and told him to watch out for a certain visitor who would arrive exhausted on the western shore of the island from Ireland in three days, whereupon the monk was to take the visitor to a house nearby to be cared for and fed. The visitor was a crane, which flew in buffeted by a storm and collapsed on the beach, almost dead. The monk lifted it tenderly and brought it to the house where he gave it food and water. When the monk returned to the monastery in the evening, the abbot commended him for his care of the guest and told him that when it was rested and restored, it would fly back to Ireland on the third day. On the third day all the monks gathered and the crane rose up in the air, circled and then headed off in the direction of Ireland.[32] This story illustrates St Columba's gift of foresight and also his affinity with the natural world.

Perhaps there is some significance in the fact that one of the most famous Irish monasteries was in Scotland. Even at this early stage in Irish Christianity, Ireland was reaching beyond herself. Culturally and spiritually, Ireland has ever since extended beyond the island of Ireland. A generation later than St Columba, his namesake St Columbanus was the most famous of the Irish pilgrims to go to the continent. He was followed by many others. So numerous were they in the seventh and eighth centuries that Dom Jean Leclercq refers to 'The Irish Invasion'.[33] They established monasteries in remote areas, which became centres of evangelisation and pastoral care. They were assiduous in preserving manuscripts and copying books, thus ensuring that the learning of the ancient world was not lost. They also practised agriculture.

In the fifth century the Roman Empire collapsed. During the three hundred years that followed, from roughly AD

500–800, civilisation struggled, with constant warfare and widespread destruction. The same period in Ireland, however, was one of peace. It was the period during which the great monasteries grew and flourished, giving Ireland its reputation as the 'island of saints and scholars'. The birth of a new European civilization in the Carolingian Empire was due to three factors. The first was the emergence of the kingdom of the Franks which eventually, after much fighting, succeeded in establishing peace. There can be no civilisation without peace and stability. The second was the papacy, which provided moral guidance, a sense of continuity and the ideal of unity. Third, there were the monasteries which preserved the learning of the ancient world. Most importantly, they evangelised the Barbarians. The major contribution to the renewal and spread of monasticism during the period was made by the Irish. It is no accident that the area encompassed by the empire of Charlemagne comprises the territories where the Irish *peregrini* worked.

The first wave of Irish missionaries in the modern period went to minister to the needs of the Irish diaspora. In the twentieth century this missionary activity was extended to evangelising new mission fields in Africa, Asia and Latin America. The contribution of Irish missionaries to the worldwide Church in the twentieth century can only be described as extraordinary. In the nineteenth century all sectors of the Irish Church had got involved in education. Now they all got involved in the missions as well. I would like to take just two examples: the Missionary Society of St Columban and the Medical Missionaries of Mary. I also mention the Legion of Mary which played an important role in the Columban mission to China.

The Missionary Society of St Columban

China is one of the oldest civilizations in the world. Christian missionaries from Persia had worked there in the seventh century and again in the thirteenth century. In the sixteenth century the Jesuits made great advances in understanding Chinese culture and had some success in bringing the Gospel to China. In the nineteenth century French missionaries had worked in the country. The Catholic Church in China was small, very small in comparison to the size of the population, but it had great potential. This situation sparked the imagination of two Irish priests, Fr Edward Galvin and Fr John Blowick. In 1916 they came up with the idea of setting up a society of secular priests in order to undertake a mission to China.[34] There had been a long tradition of Irish diocesan priests working abroad. They were either on 'temporary mission' in Britain or America, or were ordained for a diocese in Britain, America, Australia or another English-speaking country with Irish immigrants. They ministered to communities that were already Christian. The 'foreign missions' had been served by members of religious orders. So the idea of a society of secular priests with the purpose of evangelising new mission territories was a novel one in Ireland. The new society took St Columbanus as their patron and became known as the Missionary Society of St Columban.

The founders wanted the society to have its own college, which would be a headquarters for the society as well as a house of formation for students. In 1917 they leased a Georgian mansion with a farm at Dalgan Park near Shrule, County Galway. This became St Columban's College. The first students arrived in January 1918 and the Maynooth

Mission to China was set up as a diocesan society by decree of Bishop Thomas O'Dea of Galway on 28 June of that year.[35] Later the Society was to acquire Dowdstown House, with a six-hundred-acre farm attached, near Navan in County Meath. A new college was built there and opened in 1941. Saint Columban's College was moved to the new location and the name of Dalgan Park was also transferred to it.

The new society actually caught the imagination of the whole country. It got support from every parish in Ireland. *The Far East* magazine – still in publication – informed people of the aims and activities of the society, and the society went on to recruit members in Britain, America, Australia and New Zealand. Magazines were also published in these countries, so that people in parishes could be informed about the work of the society and support it with prayer and financial assistance.

The first group of Columbans – John Blowick, Edward Galvin and Owen McPolin – arrived in China in June 1920. The mission that had been entrusted to them was in Hanyang, a small city on the Yangtze River in the province of Hupeh in the central area of China. There were already some Catholics in the area and a parish structure existed. The Columbans opened more parishes, built churches and schools and trained catechists. For the first ten years the missionaries made slow progress, but in the following decade there was a remarkable growth in the membership of the Church. The Columbans were joined in their mission by three doctors, the Irish Christian Brothers, Loreto Sisters from Kentucky and the newly formed Missionary Sisters of St Columban.[36]

In 1927 Edward Galvin was ordained bishop and appointed Vicar Apostolic of Hanyang. In 1928 the Columbans took over a mission in Nancheng in the eastern part of China. French Vincentians had established parishes, schools, a seminary and an orphanage, which the Columbans then built upon. In 1946 they opened another mission in Huchow, to the north of Nancheng, while in that same year Pope Pius XII set up the Chinese hierarchy with diocesan bishops instead of vicars apostolic. This meant it was officially a local Church with its own bishops rather than a mission territory with vicars who were delegates of the pope. Edward Galvin then became Bishop of Hanyang. A number of the new bishops were Chinese and there was a growing cohort of native priests.[37]

Women played an important role in the Columban mission in China. Frances Moloney, a young widow, became interested in the work of the new society and wanted to join in its work. Fathers Blowick and Galvin realised that woman missionaries would be needed in order to minister to women and families. Frances got together twelve companions and in 1922 the Congregation of Missionary Sisters of St Columban was set up. The sisters were soon working in China, complementing the work of the priests. Bishop Galvin believed that women were the key to the future of the Church in China and that they would be its salvation. Among the Chinese Catholics there were already a number of consecrated virgins, rather like the virgins in the early Church. They took a private vow of celibacy and lived at home, while doing charitable work in the community. In 1939 Bishop Galvin organised these women into a religious congregation, the Sisters of St Mary.

They were given religious formation and some went on to train as nurses and teachers. Their role was to minister to women and girls in their own localities, especially in rural areas. Given the breakdown in law and order, it was too dangerous to send foreign sisters with no family to protect them into these areas.[38]

During the time that the Columbans worked in China the political situation was unstable. A revolution in 1911 brought an end to the Chinese empire, but it was succeeded by a situation in which various factions struggled for control of the country. Gradually the *Kuomintang* movement led by Chiang Kai Shek managed to establish itself as the government of China. This regime was favourable to Christianity. However, the Japanese invaded China in 1937 and so the country was in a state of war until 1945, when Japan was on the losing side in the Second World War. A number of Columbans were interned during the Japanese occupation. After the war China was in economic and social disarray and this gave the opportunity to the communists to emerge. Communist armies defeated the government forces and on 1 October 1949 the People's Democratic Republic of China was declared. Chiang Kai Shek and his associates fled to Taiwan.[39]

When the communists came to power in 1949 Christians and foreign missionaries, in particular, began to come under pressure. Foreign missionaries were regarded as imperialists and their activities were immediately restricted. Catholic missionaries were a particular target for harassment because of the Catholic Church's opposition to communism. Many of the Columbans were imprisoned for a time and all the priests and sisters were eventually expelled from the country.

Father Edward MacElroy was the last of the Columbans to be expelled from China in 1954.[40] The Catholic Church in China, however, continued as an underground movement, with many of its priests and laity enduring long years in prison. In recent times the Church has emerged again and is growing. One of the problems facing Catholics in China is overcoming the schism with the Chinese Catholic Patriotic Association which was set up by the government in order to exclude all foreign influence in Chinese affairs.

China had been the main focus of the Columbans from the start, but gradually they started opening missions in other Asian countries such as the Philippines (1929), Korea (1933), Burma (1936) and Japan (1948). After missionaries had been expelled from China in the 1950s, the Columbans took on missionary work among the poor in Latin America and also spread to other parts of Asia. From the start the Missionary Society of St Columban involved the wider Church in its work. Since 1960 diocesan priests have been able to work with the Columban missionaries for limited periods as associate members. The involvement of lay people was also expanded with the Columban Lay Mission Programme.[41]

The Legion of Mary

The Legion of Mary, an organisation of the lay apostolate, was founded in Dublin in 1921 by Frank Duff. It was providential that the Legion came into being around the same time as the Columbans, as it was to form an important part of their work in China. Father Aedan McGrath toured the country helping to set up *praesidia* (local branches) of the Legion of Mary.[42] The most important fruit of this work was the effect of the Legion on its own members. They became the backbone of the Church.

Many of them endured persecution and imprisonment. The Legion of Mary became a particular target of the Communist Chinese government, and on 7 October 1951 (ironically the Feast of Our Lady of the Rosary) the Legion was officially suppressed by the government, with Fr McGrath and a number of legionaries being arrested. Later more priests and more legionaries were arrested and imprisoned. The foreign priests were eventually expelled from China, but the Chinese priests and legionaries remained in prison.[43]

The Columbans in the Philippines

The Philippines had been part of the Spanish Empire from the sixteenth century until the end of the nineteenth century when it was taken over by the Americans. The country became independent in 1946. Spanish missionaries had brought Christianity to the Philippines and the great majority of the people were Catholic. However, the Spanish had neglected to adequately foster a native clergy. With the end of Spanish rule most of the Spanish clergy left the country, leaving a severe shortage of priests. In 1916 an Irishman, Michael O'Doherty, was appointed Archbishop of Manila and he appealed to the Columbans for help. Thus the Philippines became the first country outside of China to which the Columban mission expanded.

From the care of one parish in 1929 the work of the Columbans expanded to sixty-six parishes by 1954. There was a great need for religious instruction and so this became a priority. As well as establishing schools, they organised the training of catechists and various groups of lay apostolate. The Columbans were willing to tackle difficult situations and take on parishes in remote and dangerous areas.[44]

Father Rufus Halley

Michael Anthony Halley,[45] known as Rufus because of his red hair, was from Killotteran on the outskirts of Waterford City. Born in 1944, Rufus joined the Columbans in 1962 and was ordained at their college in Dalgan Park on Easter Sunday 1969. Apart from two short assignments in Ireland and Britain, he spent all of his priestly life in the Philippines.

I met Fr Rufus a number of times during his visits to Waterford. A gentle, quietly spoken person with a radiant smile, he was doing heroic work in the Philippines. Most of his time there was spent in the prelature of Marawi on the island of Mindanao. In recent years he was pastor of Malabang. Mindanao has a mixed population of Christians and Muslims. For many years a war has been going on between government forces and separatist guerrillas. There has been much misunderstanding and distrust between the Christian and Muslim communities. As well as ministering to his Christian parishioners, Rufus tried to reach out to his Muslim neighbours. In this he had a surprising degree of success. Back in the 1980s he used to spend some of his spare time working in a grocery shop owned by Muslims, as a way of meeting people. On one occasion Rufus mediated between two feuding Muslim families and succeeded in bring about reconciliation, a remarkable feat for a Catholic priest.

Rufus knew that the area in which he was working was a dangerous one. Over the years a number of priests had been kidnapped, and Rufus himself had received threats from those who did not like his work for reconciliation. He was, however, committed to his people and his ministry, with his colleagues saying that he was always positive and upbeat in his attitude. Returning home one evening in 2001 on his motorcycle, he was accosted by four masked bandits who tried to kidnap him. When he resisted they shot him dead. The outpouring of grief that followed his death showed the esteem in which Rufus had been held by the people of the region. Over two thousand people, Muslim and Christian, filed past his body at Our Lady of Peace Parish Church in Malabang. A huge throng also accompanied the cortege to Cagayan for the Funeral Mass at Immaculate Conception Parish Church. He was buried in the nearby cemetery.

Father Rufus Halley was posthumously awarded the prestigious Peace Award by the Aurora Aragon-Quezon Peace Foundation and Concerned Women of the Philippines. His brother Emmet and sister Evelyn travelled to Manila to receive the award on Rufus's behalf in February 2003. Representatives of the Muslim community in Malabang were present. Father Halley was the twenty-third member of the Missionary Society of St Columban to be killed while serving on the missions.

The Medical Missionaries of Mary

The Medical Missionaries of Mary[46] were founded by Mother Mary Martin. Coming together as a group of women in 1934, they became a religious congregation in 1937. Marie Helena Martin was born in Glenageary, County Dublin in 1892. From an early age Marie was aware of the wider world: with her family home overlooking

Dublin bay, she watched the ships coming into the port and leaving to disappear beyond the horizon. The outbreak of the First World War in 1914 brought great disruption to the Martin family as two of Marie's brothers, Tommy and Charlie, enlisted to fight in the war, as did her boyfriend, Gerald. Marie volunteered as a nurse to help tend soldiers wounded in the war. After training in Dublin, Marie was sent to Malta and later to Paris where she nursed those wounded in the battle of The Somme in 1916. Her brother Charlie was reported missing and later confirmed dead.

After the war Marie returned to Dublin and told her boyfriend that married life was not her calling. Instead she felt called to live a life of love in a different way. Through her experience of caring for the wounded, she realised that the vocation of doctors and nurses was a wonderful way of bringing the love of God to people. She trained as a midwife at the National Maternity Hospital in Holles Street, and in 1921 Marie volunteered as a lay missionary in response to an appeal by Bishop Joseph Shanahan who was working in Nigeria. She saw the great need for healthcare in Africa and realised that it could be provided by a group of dedicated religious women. Marie came up with a new idea: that of combining medical work with the missionary apostolate. She particularly wanted to help expectant mothers and babies. She returned to Ireland and set about getting other idealistic young women to help her.

One of the obstacles facing Marie was that, while there was a long tradition of nuns working as nurses, they were not permitted to be midwives or obstetricians. The other obstacle was her own health. Despite these difficulties Marie held on to her vision. During her frequent bouts of illness, she read a lot. She drew much inspiration from the writings of Dom (now Blessed) Columba Marmion. Dom Marmion was a Dublin diocesan priest who joined the Benedictine Abbey of Maredsous in Belgium and became abbot. His book *Christ, the Life of the Soul* appeared in 1916 and was an immediate success. *Christ in His Mysteries* (1919) was an extended meditation on the liturgical year. He had a fresh approach to spiritual writing, drawing on Scripture, the liturgy and theology in a way that was unusual at the time. His works are important in the history of spirituality and influenced the Liturgical Movement. Marie became interested in Benedictine spirituality and realised that the missionary society she wished to found would benefit greatly from it.

Eventually, by March 1934 Marie had got a group of women together. They took up residence in Glenstal Priory where they received formation in Benedictine spirituality from the prior Dom Bede Lebbe. Marie was matron in the secondary school run by the monks, and the group remained at Glenstal for over two years.

In 1936 approval was given for women religious to do all medical and surgical work. Marie, together with two companions, headed for Africa in December of that year, as the process to set up a new religious congregation proceeded in Rome. They went to Nigeria where Marie had found the inspiration for the new congregation twenty years earlier. However, Marie suffered a heart attack and made her profession of vows on what was thought to be her death bed on 4 April 1937. This was the Second Sunday of Easter and she took the name Sister Mary of the Incarnation.

When she recovered, Sr Mary returned to Ireland, while the other sisters remained in Nigeria. Sister Joseph Moynagh and Sr Magdalen O'Rourke did their noviciate there and were professed. The Medical Missionaries of Mary took on the work of caring for mothers and infants, which had been Mother Mary's original inspiration. They also took on the challenge of leprosy control and responded to other health needs, while also setting up hospitals and clinics. An important aspect of their work was health education and the training of nurses.

Mother Mary Martin opened a novitiate for the new congregation at Collon, County Louth, in 1938. The following year she was invited to take over a maternity home at Beechgrove in Drogheda. Drogheda was to become the motherhouse of the congregation and Mother Mary's base for the rest of her life. She died there in 1975 at Our Lady of Lourdes Hospital in the care of her own sisters. By the time of her death there were over four hundred sisters and they had missions in Nigeria, Tanzania, Uganda, Kenya, Malawi, Ethiopia, Angola and Taiwan. Mother Mary Martin visited the United States in 1950. A number of communities were established there and also in Britain in the 1960s. These also became bases of mission and of support for the work of the sisters in poor countries. Missions were later established in Brazil, Honduras, Rwanda and Benin. Many sisters now come from Africa, with houses of formation in Nigeria and Kenya.

Mother Mary Martin found her vocation in the midst of the terrible suffering caused by war. The Medical Missionaries have continued to help the victims of war, especially in the many conflicts that have occurred in Africa in the twentieth century.

NOTES

1. Jonas, *The Life of St Columban*, 9.
2. Cf. *The Divine Office* (London: Collins, 1974), vol. 2, p. 220.*
3. Cf. Genesis 28:10–17.
4. Cf. Genesis 45–50.
5. I am aware that some scholars regard this incident as not having a historical basis, but to me it has the ring of truth about it.
6. Cf. Michael Mullins, *The Gospel of John: A Commentary* (Dublin: Columba, 2003), pp 205–8.
7. Cf. Jn 7:14.
8. St Ignatius of Loyola, *The Autobiography*, ch. 1: 7–8. Cf. Ignatius of Loyola, *Spiritual Exercises and Selected Works*, George E. Ganss SJ, ed. (New York: Paulist Press, 1991).
9. St Ignatius of Loyola, *The Autobiography*, ch. 4:38–44.
10. Ignatius of Loyola, *Spiritual Exercises and Selected Works*, George E. Ganss SJ, ed. Notes, pp. 379–0.
11. Ibid., ch. 4:45–47.
12. Ibid., ch. 5:51–53.
13. Ibid., ch. 5:50.
14. Cf. Fra Anselmo M. Tommasini, *Irish Saints in Italy* (London: Sands and Company, 1937), pp. 401–3.
15. Cf. David Alton, *Pilgrim Ways Catholic Pilgrimage Sites in Britain and Ireland* (London: St Paul's, 2001), pp. 167–77.
16. Cf. Alton, *Pilgrim Ways*, pp. 205–10.
17. *Didache* 7.
18. Jn 4:13.
19. Cf. Eoin de Bhaldraithe, *The High Crosses of Moone and Castledermot* (Athy: Rainsford Publishing, 2009), p. 38.
20. Cf. www.ourladysisland.ie
21. The fifteen witnesses made depositions to an ecclesiastical commission of enquiry. These may be read in Tom Neary, *I Saw Our Lady* (Knock Shrine, 1977), pp. 141–56.
22. Cf. Apocalypse 5:11–13.
23. Cf. Leviticus 16.
24. St Patrick, *Confessio*, 1. Cf. Joseph Duffy, *Patrick in His Own Words* (Dublin: Veritas, 1975).
25. Ibid., 16.

26. Ibid., 2–3. Duffy, op. cit., pp. 12–13.
27. St Adomnán, *The Life of Columba*, Preface.
28. Pilgrimage is also an important theme in Russian spirituality. Cf. Catherine de Hueck Doherty, Poustinia (Glasgow: Fountain Books, 1977), pp. 36, 46.
29. Cf. Brian Lacey, *Saint Columba*, p. 43.
30. St Adomnán, *The Life of Columba*, Preface.
31. Cf. Reginald B. Hale, *The Magnificent Gael* (Ottawa, 1976), p. 116.
32. St Adomnán, *The Life of Columba*, Book 1.
33. Dom Jean Leclercq, 'From St Gregory to St Bernard', *A History of Christian Spirituality, Volume II: The Spirituality of the Middle Ages,* Jean Leclercq, Francois Vandenbroucke and Louis Bouyer (London: Burns & Oats, 1986), pp. 31–45.
34. Cf. Missionary Society of St Columban website: www.columban.com
35. Neil Collins, *The Splendid Cause: The Missionary Society of St Columban 1916–1954* (Dublin: The Columba Press, 2006), p. 52.
36. Collins, *Splendid Cause*, p. 86.
37. Ibid., p. 132.
38. Ibid., p. 128–9.
39. Stephen Neill, *A History of Christian Missions* (Harmondsworth: Penguin Books, 1964), pp. 465–7.
40. Collins, *Splendid Cause*, p. 185.
41. Cf. www.columban.com
42. Collins, *Splendid Cause*, p. 164.
43. Ibid., p. 184–5.
44. Ibid., p. 223.
45. This account of Fr Halley is based on material from the archives of the Missionary Society of St Columban, courtesy of Ms Niamh Collins.
46. Cf. Medical Missionaries of Mary website: www.mmmworldwide.org; *Celebrating 70 Years on Mission* (MMM Communications, 2007).

CHAPTER THREE

THE WISDOM TRADITION: LEARNING FROM THE EXPERIENCE OF THE COMMUNITY

The wisdom books of the Bible are usually listed as Job, Proverbs, Ecclesiastes, Ecclesiasticus and Wisdom. The Song of Songs and the Psalms are also included in this section of the Bible. Concerned with right living, wisdom literature directed that the wise person is one who has learned to live rightly, both at a theoretical and a practical level. This, of course, could be said to be the concern of the whole Bible, but what distinguishes wisdom literature is its approach. Wisdom is based on experience. The sage has reflected on human life and formulated sayings which encapsulate the insight arrived at. Thus the sage is in a position to teach others the art of right living. Because it is shared and passed on from one generation to the next, originally in oral form and then in writing, it is more than the wisdom of particular sages, it is the wisdom of the community and we may speak of a wisdom tradition.

The wisdom tradition of Israel probably has its origins in the tribal society of the period of the Judges or earlier. Young people would have been taught wise sayings and village elders would have passed on the fruits of their life's experience. In the period of the monarchy of David and Solomon, the tradition received an impetus. With worship and government centred in Jerusalem, the royal court also became a centre for wisdom, as had been the case in Egypt and Mesopotamia since the third millennium BC.[1] The Book of Proverbs is traditionally attributed to Solomon. This is like the attribution of the Psalms to David. It shows that the royal court was a setting where the teaching of wisdom was cultivated.[2]

The cultivation of wisdom continued throughout the Old Testament period. As with other parts of the Bible, the need to preserve the tradition in writing was felt particularly at the Exile and after it. The writing of wisdom books continued with Sirach in the second century BC and Wisdom in the first century BC, most likely the last book in the Old Testament to be written.[3]

The Words of the Wise

Wisdom is presented as the good advice that a loving parent gives to a young person:

> Hear, my child, your father's instruction,
> and do not reject your mother's teaching;
> for they are a fair garland for your head,
> and pendants for your neck. (Prov 1:8-9)

> My child, from your youth choose discipline,
> and when you have grey hair you will still find wisdom. (Eccles [Sir] 6:18)

The way of wisdom is the way of virtue and those who follow it find life and happiness:

> Wisdom will come into your heart
> and knowledge will be pleasant to your soul;

prudence will watch over you;
and understanding will guard you.
It will save you from the way of evil.
(Prov 2:10-12)

A wise person will have praise heaped upon him,
and all who see him will call him happy.
The days of a person's life are numbered,
but the days of Israel are without number.
One who is wise among his people will inherit honour,
and his name will live for ever.
(Eccles [Sir] 37:24-26)

Much of the advice relates to practical issues such as the wise use of money:

Do not be one of those who give pledges,
who become surety for debts.
If you have nothing with which to pay,
why should your bed be taken from under you?
(Prov 22:26-27)

Do not become a beggar by feasting with borrowed money
when you have nothing in your purse.
(Eccles [Sir] 18:33)

Wisdom is concerned with respect for parents and those in authority. It points out the consequences of developing bad habits and teaches appropriate social behaviour:

Do not be among winebibbers,
or among gluttonous eaters of meat;
for the drunkard and glutton will come to poverty,
and drowsiness will clothe them with rags.
(Prov 23:20-21)

Eat what is set before you like a well-bred person,
and do not chew greedily, or you will give offence.
Be the first to stop, as befits good manners,
and do not be insatiable, or you will give offence.
(Eccles [Sir] 31:16-17)

Above all, the acquisition of wisdom has to do with the development of character, with becoming a virtuous person. Gentleness and humility are among the virtues that are encouraged:

My child, perform your tasks with humility;
then you will be loved by those whom God accepts.
The greater you are, the more you must humble yourself;
so you will find favour in the sight of the Lord.
(Eccles [Sir] 3:17-20)

The reward for humility and fear of the Lord
is riches and honour and life. (Prov 22:4)

The Wisdom of God

The fear of the Lord is the basic attitude of the religious person.[4] It is the attitude of adoration, of recognising that God is God and of submission to his will. This attitude is fundamental for those who seek to be wise:

> The fear of the Lord is the beginning of knowledge;
> fools despise wisdom and instruction. (Prov 1:7)

> To fear the Lord is the beginning of wisdom ...
> To fear the Lord is the fullness of wisdom ...
> The fear of the Lord is the crown of wisdom;
> making peace and perfect health to flourish.
> To fear the Lord is the root of wisdom,
> and her branches are long life. (Eccles [Sir] 1:14, 16, 18, 20)

As the tradition develops it is clear that wisdom is a gift from God:

> For the Lord gives wisdom;
> from his mouth come knowledge and understanding. (Prov 2:6)

> I prayed, and understanding was given me;
> I called on God, and the spirit of wisdom came to me. (Wis 7:7)

Not only is wisdom a gift from God, but it is an attribute of God himself which is shared with the wise person:

> She [Wisdom] is a breath of the power of God,
> and a pure emanation of the glory of the Almighty
> ...
> In every generation she passes into holy souls,
> and makes them friends of God and prophets;
> for God loves nothing so much as the person who lives with wisdom. (Wis 7:25, 27-28)

The personification of wisdom is a device that safeguards the transcendence of God and at the same time shows his intimate involvement in creation:[5]

> The Lord created me at the beginning of his work,
> the first of his acts of long ago.
> I was beside him, like a master worker;
> and I was daily his delight,
> rejoicing before him always. (Prov 8:22, 30)

The wisdom of God is particularly evident in the beauty and order of creation:

> The Lord by wisdom founded the earth;
> by understanding he established the heavens;
> by his knowledge the deeps broke open,
> and the clouds drop down the dew.
> (Prov 3:19-20)

> Do you know when the mountain goats give birth?
> Do you observe the calving of the deer?

Their young ones become strong, they grow up in the open;
they go forth and do not return to them.
Is it at your command that the eagle mounts up
And makes its nest on high? (Job 39:1, 4, 27)

Wisdom and the Law

How does this tradition of wisdom relate to the Law and the Covenant? At first it appears to be distinct from the Law. It makes no claim to be directly revealed by God as the Law does. It is part of a tradition which is wider than that of Israel. Similar collections of wisdom sayings are to be found throughout the ancient near east.[6] However, for the Hebrew sages the faith of Israel is always in the background. The Covenant is the context within which the wise person will live. The wise person submits to the Law. Ben Sira teaches that true wisdom is to be found in the observance of the Law. Wisdom, understanding and discipline are all to be found in the Law of Moses.

All this is the book of the covenant of the Most High God,
the Law that Moses commanded us
as an inheritance for the congregations of Jacob.
It overflows, like the Pishon, with wisdom,
and like the Tigris at the time of the first fruits.
(Eccles [Sir] 24:23, 25)

> The Law of the Lord is perfect,
> reviving the soul;
> the decrees of the Lord are sure,
> making wise the simple. (Ps 19:7)

In fact the moral values enjoined by the Law are the same values that are commended by the wisdom tradition. It is a difference of presentation. Where the Law provides rules and sanctions, wisdom appeals to good sense and to the heart.

Wisdom in the New Testament

Not only does the wisdom tradition span the Old Testament, it is also to be found in the New Testament, for example, in the Sermon on the Mount, in the writings of St Paul and in the Letter of James.

The Sermon on the Mount

In the Sermon on the Mount (Mt 5–7) Jesus is depicted as the new and greater Moses giving the New Law. He is also the wisdom teacher *par excellence*.[7] Like the sages of the Old Testament, Jesus addresses the question of how to live rightly. In the Beatitudes Jesus presents us with the formula for true happiness. They are truly blessed who follow the values which he puts forward:

> Blessed are the poor in spirit, for theirs is the kingdom of heaven.
> Blessed are those who mourn, for they will be comforted.
> Blessed are the meek, for they will inherit the earth.

> Blessed are those who hunger and thirst for righteousness,
> for they will be filled. (Mt 5:3-6)

The other beatitudes relate to mercy, purity of heart, making peace and enduring persecution. The Beatitudes are, in fact, wisdom sayings rather like the proverbs found in the wisdom books and particularly in the Psalms.[8] Each one of them contains a depth of meaning that only reveals itself when it has been reflected upon for some time. For instance, how can those who mourn be called blessed or happy? This must be a kind of happiness that runs deeper than particular states of feeling, that can co-exist with suffering. It could be said that all the beatitudes flow from the first one, which promises the kingdom of heaven to the poor in spirit. The poor in spirit are the humble, those who recognise their total dependence on God. So humility is a basic attitude of those who would enter the kingdom.

The Sermon goes on to deal with specific issues such as killing and anger, adultery, divorce, swearing, revenge and loving one's neighbour. On each of these Jesus revises the Mosaic Law, placing the emphasis on the inner attitude from which external behaviour flows. What Jesus lays down is more demanding. For instance, where Moses forbade killing, Jesus goes further and forbids anger and quarrelling. Where Moses lays down that revenge be proportionate, 'an eye for an eye', Jesus rules out revenge altogether.

The Sermon gives the teaching of Jesus on the traditional pious practices of almsgiving, prayer and fasting (cf. Mt 6:1-18). Again the emphasis is on sincerity. It is significant that Matthew includes them here in the middle of Jesus' principal moral discourse. There is no separation between morality and spirituality; both concern the whole of life.

The rest of the Sermon on the Mount contains many wise sayings of Jesus, which give insight into life. Like the Beatitudes, they are nuggets of wisdom, which repay time spent in meditation on them. Though they are very familiar, it is worthwhile giving some examples:

> No one can serve two masters; for a slave will either hate the one and love the other, or be devoted to the one and despise the other. You cannot serve God and wealth. (Mt 6:24)
>
> Is not life more than food, and the body more than clothing? (Mt 6:25)
>
> Do not judge, so that you may not be judged. For with the judgement you make you will be judged, and the measure you give will be the measure you get. (Mt 7:1-2)
>
> Do not give what is holy to dogs; and do not throw your pearls before swine, or they will trample them under foot and maul you. (Mt 7:6)
>
> In everything do to others as you would have them do to you; for this is the law and the prophets. (Mt 7:12)
>
> Enter through the narrow gate; for the gate is wide and the road is easy that leads to destruction, and there are many who take it. (Mt 7:13)

These sayings of the Lord bear a striking affinity to the proverbs of the wisdom books. Some examples from these will help illustrate the similarity:

> One who loves gold will not be justified;
> one who pursues money will be led astray by it.
> (Eccles [Sir] 31:5)

> A generous person will be enriched,
> and one who gives water will get water.
> (Prov 11:25)

> Do not speak in the hearing of a fool,
> who will only despise the wisdom of your words.
> (Prov 23:9)

> The way of sinners is paved with smooth stones,
> but at its end is the pit of Hades. (Eccles [Sir] 21:10)

The sayings of Jesus are more profound, but we can see that he is in the tradition of the sages of Israel. He has brought the wisdom tradition to its highest point, just as he has completed the Law and the Prophets.

Saint Paul

Saint Paul relates the idea of wisdom to the Paschal Mystery:[9]

> We proclaim Christ crucified ... Christ the power and the wisdom of God. (1 Cor 1:23-24)

Saint Paul contrasts this wisdom to that of the philosophers, because it is only accessible to those who have faith:

> We speak God's wisdom, secret and hidden, which God decreed before the ages for our glory. None of the rulers of this age have understood this; for if they had, they would not have crucified the Lord of glory. (1 Cor 2:7-8)

All of St Paul's letters give advice on how to live the Christian life. In some he deals with quite complicated moral issues, such as the problems arising in marriages between Christians and pagans.[10] His most extensive treatment is in Romans 12–15. This moral section of the letter follows the doctrinal section of the first eleven chapters. For St Paul, the demands of Christian living flow from what God has done for us in Christ. The moral teaching is in the form of an exhortation or *paraclesis*. A fine example of early Christian catechesis,[11] its central theme is love. Saint Paul spells out what he means by 'genuine love' or 'love without pretence'.[12]

> Let love be genuine; hate what is evil, hold fast to what is good; love one another with mutual affection; outdo one another in showing honour. Do not lag in zeal, be ardent in spirit, serve the Lord. Rejoice in hope, be patient in suffering, persevere in prayer. Contribute to the needs of the saints; extend hospitality to strangers. (Rm 12:9-13)

The letter also relates love to the Decalogue, stating that all the commandments are summed up in the commandment to love our neighbour (cf. Rm 13:9). Saint Paul's moral teaching is based on that of Jesus. Some of the sayings may go back to the Lord himself.[13] The affinity of this teaching with the wisdom tradition can be seen in the following passage. It contains echoes of Proverbs and is also very similar to it in style. Arranging the text in sayings helps to highlight this:

> Bless those who persecute you;
> bless and do not curse them.
>
> Rejoice with those who rejoice
> weep with those who weep.
>
> Live in harmony with one another;
> do not be haughty, but associate with the lowly.
>
> Do not claim to be wiser than you are.
>
> Do not repay anyone evil for evil,
> but take thought for what is noble in the sight of all.
>
> If it is possible, so far as it depends on you, live peaceably with all. (Rm 12:14-18)

The Letter of James

The Letter of James envisages a significant role for the teacher of Christian living:

> Who is wise and understanding among you? Show by your good life that your works are done with gentleness born of wisdom. (Jas 3:13)

The Letter of James is mostly concerned with moral issues. The author deals with perseverance in the face of trials, giving equal treatment to the poor and having faith that is expressed in doing good. He also gives advice on control of the tongue, unity in the community and prayer. Saint James teaches that jealousy, ambition, disharmony and wicked deeds come from an earthly attitude which is the opposite of wisdom (Jas 3: 15-16). By contrast there is the wisdom that comes from God:

> The wisdom which is from above is first pure, then peaceable, gentle, willing to yield, full of mercy and good fruits, without a trace of partiality or hypocrisy. (Jas 3:17)

Control of the tongue is a frequent theme of the wisdom literature. It is a topic that St James dwells on with graphic examples:

> Anyone who makes no mistakes in speaking is perfect, able to keep the whole body in check with a bridle. If we put bits into the mouths of horses to make them obey us, we guide their whole bodies. Or look at ships: though they are so large that it takes strong winds to guide them, yet they are guided by a very small rudder wherever the will of the pilot directs. So also the tongue is a small member, yet it boasts of great exploits. (Jas 3:2-5)

The Wisdom Tradition Continued

The approach to the Christian life that I have described above is continued in the history of the Church. I will take three examples, from different periods, of spiritual guides who, in their writings, have left us wisdom for living. These are St Benedict, St Thomas Aquinas and St Francis de Sales.

Saint Benedict

Monastic rules are among the best examples of post-biblical wisdom literature. Saint Benedict wrote the famous *Rule for Monasteries* some years before his death in 547.[14] It is no accident that the opening of the Rule of Benedict echoes Proverbs:

> Listen, my son, to your master's precepts, and incline the ear of your heart. Receive willingly and carry out effectively your loving father's advice.[15]

In Chapter Four, 'What Are the Instruments of Good Works', it is clear that the advice is first of all the keeping of the commandments. The chapter consists of a long list of practical admonitions mostly drawn from the Old and New Testaments. Here is the opening section:

> In the first place, to love the Lord God with the whole heart, the whole soul, the whole strength. Then, one's neighbour as oneself. Then not to murder. Not to commit adultery. Not to steal. Not to covet. Not to bear false witness. To respect all men. And not to do to another what one would not have done to oneself.[16]

The whole Rule is imbued with a spirit of moderation conducive to gentleness. This also characterises the monks' relationships with each other:

> They should anticipate one another in honour; most patiently endure one another's infirmities, whether of body or of character; vie in paying obedience to one another.[17]

St Benedict devotes a whole chapter to humility. Taking the analogy of Jacob's ladder, he describes twelve degrees of humility by which the monk ascends to God. Paradoxically, what appears to be the descent of humility is in fact an ascent. Humility is a whole spiritual programme for St Benedict. It includes practising mindfulness of God, turning from self-will and enduring difficulties patiently. Humility involves having a modest opinion of oneself and expresses itself in obedience to superiors, observance of the Rule, in keeping silent and even in one's outward demeanour. At the end of the chapter he tells us what humility achieves:

> Having climbed all these steps of humility, therefore, the monk will presently come to that perfect love of God which casts out fear. And all those precepts which formerly he had not observed without fear, he will now begin to keep by reason of that love, without any effort, as though naturally and by habit.[18]

Saint Thomas Aquinas

Saint Thomas Aquinas began writing the *Summa Theologiae* in 1265 or shortly afterwards, and it remained unfinished at his death in 1274.[19] The *Summa* is divided into three parts. Morality, which is considered in the Second Part, is set within the broad context of God's plan of salvation, beginning with God and Creation in the First Part and concluding with Christ and Redemption in the Third Part. In the Second Part, St Thomas first considers human destiny and morality in general terms beginning with happiness,[20] and then goes on to deal with the particular demands of moral living in terms of the virtues.[21]

Saint Thomas tells us that there is the wisdom which is a virtue and also the wisdom which is a gift of the Holy Spirit.

> A correct judgement made through rational investigation belongs to the wisdom which is an intellectual virtue. But to judge aright through a certain fellowship with them belongs to that wisdom which is a gift of the Holy Spirit ... Now this sympathy, or connaturality with divine things, results from charity which unites us to God.[22]

Wisdom as a gift of the Holy Spirit is present in all who have charity.[23] Through faith and charity we are children of God and share in the gift of wisdom.

> Now men are called children of God in so far as they participate in the likeness of his only begotten and natural Son ... who is Wisdom Begotten. So

> in receiving the gift of wisdom a man enters into the state of being a child of God.[24]

Saint Thomas interprets the personification of wisdom in Wisdom 7:27 as referring to God the Son.

> That text refers to Uncreated Wisdom who first joins us to himself by the gift of love and reveals mysteries to us from that love.[25]

As we have seen, the biblical wisdom tradition was much concerned with the practical issues involved in the art of right living. Saint Thomas agrees that wisdom guides not only theory, but practice as well.[26] In fact it enhances all that we do.

> The guidance of human acts by wisdom does not bring bitterness or toil; rather by wisdom the bitter becomes sweet and the toil a rest.[27]

Like St James, St Thomas sees wisdom as particularly associated with peace.

> Peace results from putting things in the proper order which is what wisdom does. This corresponds to the seventh beatitude which promises that the peacemakers will be called children of God.[28]

Let us take two short examples of St Thomas's remarks on practical issues which show his good sense and his consistency with the wisdom tradition.

> External goods are required for the imperfect happiness open to us in this life, not that they lie at the heart of happiness, yet they are tools to serve happiness which lies in the activity of virtue.[29]

> If we speak of present-life happiness and agree with Aristotle, then the happy man must have friends. It is not that he makes use of them, since he is self-contained, or because he finds them pleasant, since he finds his pleasure in the activity of virtue, but that he needs them in order that he may act well, namely that he may do them good, that he may take delight in seeing them do good, and also that they may help him in his good works, for he needs their support in both the active and the contemplative life.[30]

Saint Francis de Sales

Saint Francis de Sales wrote *Introduction to the Devout Life* as a book of advice for lay people wanting to live a fully committed Christian life in the world. Originally compiled for private circulation, a first edition of this work was published in 1609 and a revised and expanded final edition appeared in 1619.[31] This is usually regarded as a spiritual book, but it is not limited to advice on prayer and the sacraments. It includes a full programme of Christian living. The third section entitled 'The Practice of Virtue' covers such topics as relationships, marriage, friendship, pastimes, money, conversation and doing one's duty. Spirituality and morality are not separated.

There are three chapters on humility in *Introduction to the Devout Life*. He warns against false humility, of pretending that we have no good points or talents. We should rather acknowledge that these are gifts with which God has favoured us. He says: 'nothing can so humble us before God's mercy as the multitude of his favours.'[32] In the chapter on gentleness, St Francis tells us that 'Humility perfects our relationship with God, gentleness our relationship with our neighbour.'[33]

Unlike some other spiritual writers of his time, St Francis de Sales had a high regard for friendship. While he distinguishes between true and false friendship, and warns against the dangers of the latter, he sees true friendship as an aid to fostering the Christian life.

> Let your charity extend to everyone, Philothea, but limit your friendship to those with whom you can share virtuous things; the more perfect you are, the more perfect will your friendship be.[34]

> It is necessary for those who seek true virtue in the world to form good and holy friendships, to encourage, help and guide one another on the path of virtue.[35]

The Irish Oral Tradition

An aspect of Irish culture very similar to that of ancient Israel is that of the *seanfhocail* or proverbs which are handed on from one generation to the next.[36] Some of these wisdom sayings concern life in general. Others have a moral message, while a number of sayings are religious in character. In the oral culture of the past they had an important role in teaching the young. They are still valuable nuggets of wisdom and give us an insight into the outlook of our forbears. Some of them are also heard in English or have English equivalents.

Examples of sayings concerning life in general are the following:

> *Is binn béal ina thost.* The silent mouth is sweet/ Silence is golden.

> *Ní thagann ciall ach le aois.* Sense only comes with age.

Some sayings are based on observations of the natural world applied to human life. Two examples show this.

> *Briseann an dúchas tré shúile an chait.* Nature breaks out through the eyes of the cat. (Meaning: People tend to have the same character traits as their parents.)

> *Ní féidir leis an gobadán an dá thrá a fhreastail.* The sandpiper cannot serve two strands. (Meaning: Two jobs cannot be done at the same time. No one can serve two masters.)

The following are examples of moral proverbs.

> *Ar scáth a chéile a mhaireann na daoine.* It is in each other's shade that people live. (Meaning: People depend on each other.)

> *Filleann an feall ar an feallaire.* The evil deed returns to the evildoer.

The first of these examples shows a stress on the value of community and the second a belief in justice.

Religious proverbs often express faith in the goodness of God, such as these:

> *Tá Dia maith agus tá Máthair mhaith aige.* God is good and he has a good Mother.
> *Is giorra cabhair Dé ná an doras.* God's help is nearer than the door.

There is also a trust in divine providence, as in these examples.

> *Níor dhún Dia doras riamh, nár oscail sé ceann eile.* God never closed one door without opening another.

> *Labhair Dia romhat.* God spoke before you. (Meaning: What appears to be bad news, may turn out for the best.)

The great value placed on Mass is also an important theme in the traditional sayings, as in this example:

> *Aifreann Domhnaigh ná lig tharat pé fliuch, fuar, a bheidh an lá.* Do not miss Sunday Mass, however wet or cold the day.

The Relevance of the Wisdom Tradition for Today

The wisdom tradition continues today. It is the handing on of values, which is vital to the life of the Church, as it is to all human society. The Church is the great repository of the wisdom the Bible and of the subsequent tradition of Christian living. The Church has the primary task of forming people in the Christian life. She does this through preaching, liturgy and catechesis. In the lives of the saints she holds up examples to us of how to put the Gospel into practice. The teaching authority of the Church also has the role of confronting new questions that arise, and of applying to them the wisdom that has been built up and handed down. The social teaching of the Church and the encyclicals of the popes on the various issues that arise are a rich source of wisdom for today.

Moral theology and moral catechesis have in the past mostly used the legal model of the Old Testament, specifically the Decalogue. The wisdom model complements this. It emphasises the positive demands of good living rather than the prohibitions of the law. The wisdom approach to moral instruction is the handing on within the community of the fruits of experience reflected upon in the light of faith. Its purpose is to give encouragement and guidance to the young and to all those looking for help in following the right path in life. The Second Vatican Council encouraged the renewal of moral theology and called for a renewed contact with Sacred Scripture.[37] The wisdom literature of the Old Testament is the most neglected part of the Bible. Yet it has had an important influence on the New Testament, and the approach to moral teaching that it represents is potentially a very fruitful one.

Presenting the Church's moral teaching as wisdom for living is much more appealing than presenting it in terms of what is permitted and what is forbidden. It comes across as helping people, rather than trying to coerce them. It appeals to their own sense of what is good and right. The New Testament approach to morality is much more than delineating the limits of what is permitted. It is a constant call to a more generous response to what God has done for us in Christ. The wisdom tradition, biblical, post-biblical and ongoing, in the life of the Church is a rich source for guiding that response.

NOTES

1. Lawrence E. Boadt CSP, 'An Introduction to the Wisdom Literature of Israel', *The Collegeville Bible Commentary*, Dianne Bergant CSA and Robert J. Karris OFM, general eds (Collegeville, Minnesota: The Liturgical Press, 1989), pp. 635–6.
2. Gerhard von Rad, *Wisdom in Israel* (London: SCM Press Ltd., 1972), pp. 15–16.
3. Boadt, op. cit., pp. 640–41.
4. Von Rad, *Wisdom in Israel*, p. 66.
5. Boadt, op. cit., p. 642. Cf. Von Rad, *Wisdom in Israel*, pp. 144–57.
6. Boadt CSP, op. cit., pp. 635–6.
7. Wilfrid J. Harrington OP, *Matthew: Sage Theologian* (Dublin: The Columba Press, 1998), p. 108.
8. John L. McKenzie SJ, *Dictionary of the Bible* (London: Geoffrey Chapman, 1965), p. 84. Cf. Daniel J. Harrington SJ, 'Matthew' *The Collegeville Bible Commentary*, pp. 869–70.
9. The Paschal Mystery and its implications for spirituality are discussed more fully in Chapter Six.
10. E.g. 1 Corinthians 7:12–16.
11. Michael Mullins, *Called to be Saints* (Dublin: Veritas, 1991), p. 201.
12. *hê agapê anhypokritos.*
13. Mullins, *Called to be Saints*, p. 204.

14. Dom Justin McCann, *Saint Benedict* (London: Sheed and Ward, 1937), p. 205 and p. 210.
15. Rule of St Benedict, Prologue. *St Benedict's Rule for Monasteries* Leonard J. Doyle, trans., p. 1.
16. RB, 4. Op. cit., p. 14.
17. RB, 72. Op. cit., p. 99.
18. RB, 7. Op. cit., pp. 28–9.
19. James A. Weisheipl, *Friar Thomas d'Aquino* (Oxford: Basil Blackwell, 1974), p. 221 and p. 327.
20. *Prima Secundae.*
21. *Secunda Secundae.*
22. Saint Thomas Aquinas, *Summa Theologiae*, 2a 2ae, q. 45, 2, response, Blackfriars edition, Thomas Gilby OP STM, general ed. (London: Eyre & Spottiswood, 1972), vol. 35, p. 167.
23. *Summa Theologiae*, 1a 2ae, q. 68, 5, ad 1. Op. cit., vol. 24, p. 27.
24. *Summa Theologiae*, 2a 2ae, q. 45, 6, resp. Op. cit., vol. 35, p. 177.
25. *Summa Theologiae*, 2a 2ae, q. 45, 6, ad 2. Op. cit., vol. 35, p. 177.
26. *Summa Theologiae*, 2a 2ae, q. 45, 4, sed con. Op. cit., vol. 35, p. 169.
27. *Summa Theologiae*, 2a 2ae, q. 45, 4, ad 3. Op. cit., vol. 35, p. 169.
28. *Summa Theologiae*, 2a 2ae, q. 45, 6, resp. Op. cit., vol. 35, p. 177.
29. *Summa Theologiae*, 1a 2ae, q. 4, 7, resp. Op. cit., vol. 16, p. 111.
30. *Summa Theologiae*, 1a 2ae, q. 4, 8, resp. Op. cit., vol. 16, p. 113.
31. Saint Francis de Sales, *Introduction to the Devout Life*, Michael Day, Cong. Orat., trans. (London: Burns & Oats, 1962), Translator's Note, p. v.
32. Ibid., p. 100.
33. Ibid., p. 111.
34. Ibid., p. 139.
35. Ibid., p. 140.
36. I am indebted to Eibhlín Bean Uí Dhonnachadha of An Rinn for providing me with the seanfhocail in this account of the Irish tradition of proverbs.
37. *Optatam Totius*, no. 16.

CHAPTER FOUR

THE PROPHETS: WITNESSES TO GOD'S WORD

Who are the Prophets?

The prophet is a significant figure in the Bible. In the stories where they feature, prophets usually burst upon the scene and their interventions are usually dramatic. Take for instance the Prophet Nathan. King David has just pulled a fast one as he sees it. He has seduced the wife of Uriah the Hittite and then arranged to have Uriah himself killed. He is quite satisfied with himself. Then Nathan suddenly appears and tells him the story of the man who has no compassion. David is outraged and declares that the man deserves to die. Nathan delivers the decisive blow: 'You are the man' (2 Sm 12:1-15). The prophet is often a thorn in the side of the authorities. King Ahab was not happy when he saw the Prophet Elijah coming. It usually meant he was going to be taken to task for some wrongdoing.[1]

The Hebrew Prophets

The Jewish or Hebrew Bible is traditionally divided into three sections: the Law, the Prophets and the Writings. Included in the Prophets are a number of books, which in the Christian Bible are placed among the Historical Books. Joshua, Judges, Samuel and Kings, each treated as a single book, are the Early Prophets. The Later Prophets are Isaiah, Jeremiah, Ezekiel and the Minor Prophets or 'the Twelve', as they are known. Daniel, is not included in the Prophets, but placed with the Writings. These books cover the classical period of Hebrew prophecy. The earlier works give us much information about the lives of such prophets as Samuel and Elijah, as well as giving us the historical background. The later works give us the writings of the prophets themselves. The arrangement of the Hebrew Bible underlines the significance of the prophets as providing a commentary on the Law, at the heart of which is the Mosaic Covenant. In the Christian Bible the earlier prophets are placed with the Historical Books, as mentioned above, while the later prophets are placed after the Wisdom Books (the Writings of the Hebrew Bible). This arrangement means that the prophets immediately precede the New Testament. The prophets are seen as pointing to the New Testament, at the heart of which is the person of Jesus.

In the creed we say that the Holy Spirit is the one who spoke through the prophets. This expresses well what the vocation of the prophet is. A prophet is one through whom God speaks. Prophecy is a gift of the Holy Spirit, a charism. Moses is the prophet *par excellence*, but he is not typical of the prophets. Moses was more than a prophet. He was also the mediator of the covenant between God and the Israelites. We meet the more typical prophet in the prophetic books of the Bible. The Hebrew prophets were conscious of having received messages from God which they passed on to the people. In them we see clearly what this particular gift of the Holy Spirit is about. Prophecy, however, is not confined to the period of the great Hebrew prophets. The writers of the New Testament were aware that the Holy Spirit was speaking, not only through Jesus, but through those who spoke in his name. There are also people through whom God speaks who are not necessarily conscious of having received a revelation. They feel moved to speak out about a particular issue or their lives have a message for the people of their time. The Holy Spirit is also working through these people and inspiring what they say. In this way, and also in more dramatic ways, the charism of prophecy has continued to be present throughout the history of the Church. In this chapter I want to reflect on the gift of prophecy as it has been found in the Bible and also in the life of the Church.

The Calling of the Prophet

Prophecy in Israel was not a permanent institution like priesthood or kingship. A prophet could come from anywhere. A prophet could be male or female. There were women prophets like Deborah. Although all the prophets had certain characteristics in common, every prophet was unique. Each one was raised up by God to address a particular situation at a particular time. Every prophet received a vocation or call. Perhaps the most dramatic example of this is the call of Samuel. Samuel was given over to the Lord by his mother Hannah at an early age and put into the care of Eli, priest of Shiloh. At night he hears a voice calling his name and runs to Eli to see what he wants. Eli tells him to go back to sleep. This happens three times before Eli realises that the child is hearing a voice from God. He then tells him to say, 'Speak, Lord, your servant is listening', the next time the voice speaks. From then on Samuel was in direct communication with the Almighty.

The story is rounded off with the wonderful phrase, 'and Samuel let no word of his fall to the ground' (1 Sm 3: 1-19).

Jeremiah also experienced the call of God as a young man and, in fact, God told him that this had been his destiny since before his conception.

> Before I formed you in the womb I knew you,
> Before you were born I consecrated you;
> I appointed you a prophet to the nations. (Jer 1:3)

Jeremiah expresses a certain reluctance or sense of inadequacy at such a prospect, but the Lord assures him that he will be with him and, in a phrase that expresses the prophet's relationship to the word, God says: 'Now, I have put my words in your mouth' (Jer 1:9).

Isaiah is also keenly aware of his inadequacy and unworthiness, when he experiences God's call during the liturgy in the temple. In this instance the experience is initially described as seeing rather than hearing.

> I saw the Lord sitting on a throne, high and lofty; and the hem of his robe filled the temple. Seraphs were in attendance above him; each had six wings: with two they covered their faces, and with two they covered their feet, and with two they flew. And one called to another and said: 'Holy, holy, holy is the Lord of hosts; the whole earth is full of his glory.' (Is 6: 1-3)

The Mission of the Prophet

The mission of the prophet is to bring God's Word to the people. The sending of a prophet is a sending of the Lord's Word. In fact, the prophets are all convinced that what they proclaim is not their own word but the Word of the Lord. When God is about to intervene in a particular situation by sending a prophet, this is often introduced by saying that 'the Word of the Lord came to' that particular prophet. The prophet has been chosen by God to be his spokesperson. The word spoken by the prophet is the Word of God. The prophet often prefaces his message with, 'Thus says the Lord' or a similar phrase. Here are some examples of the identification of the prophetic word with the divine word.

> Now Elijah the Tishbite of Tishbe in Gilead, said to Ahab, 'As the Lord the God of Israel lives, before whom I stand, there shall be neither dew nor rain these years, except by my word'. (1 Kgs 17:1)

> Hear, O heavens, and listen, O earth; for the Lord has spoken. (Is 1:2)

> But neither he [King Zedekiah] nor his servants nor the people of the land listened to the word of the Lord that he spoke through the prophet Jeremiah. (Jer 37:2)

The Psychological Experiences of the Prophets

Although people sometimes consulted the prophet, there was an essential difference between the Hebrew Prophets and the mediums, seers and soothsayers of other religions. Whereas mediums and other spiritual practitioners tried to make contact with the Divinity, the world of spirits or the dead, the prophets did not do this. The Word of God came to them. It was always God who took the initiative. The true God was not to be manipulated. The question arises as to how this happened. In the prophetic literature we read about the Word of the Lord coming to the prophet and the Lord speaking through the prophet. We also read about the prophet hearing and seeing. What does all this mean?

It would seem that God communicated with the prophets through visions, auditions and inspired thoughts.[2] Auditions could be either external, in which case the prophet heard an actual voice speaking, or internal. The visions and auditions would appear to have come to the prophet suddenly and unexpectedly.[3] They did not work themselves into a state of heightened consciousness in order to receive a revelation. There would, however, have been some kind of alteration of consciousness during the experience.

The Prophet Elisha would appear to have been a visionary.[4] The reference to the prophet fixing his gaze and staring indicates some kind of trance in which Elisha saw a vision of the future. Isaiah was also a visionary. His call was in the form of a vision. He also had a vision of the fall of Babylon. This vision was not a pleasant experience. The prophet is distressed at what he sees:

> A stern vision is told to me: the betrayer betrays,
> and the destroyer destroys.
> Go up, O Elam, lay siege, O Media; all the sighing
> she has caused I bring to an end.

> Therefore my loins are filled with anguish; pangs have seized me, like the pangs of a woman in labour; I am bowed down so that I cannot hear, I am dismayed so that I cannot see.
> My mind reels, horror has appalled me; the twilight I longed for has been turned for me into trembling. (Is 21:2-4)

Amos has a series of visions and God interprets the visions for him. Here is one of them:

> This is what the Lord God showed me: a basket of summer fruit. He said, 'Amos, what do you see?' And I said, 'A basket of summer fruit.' Then the Lord said to me, 'The end has come upon my people Israel; I will never again pass them by. The songs of the temple shall become wailings on that day,' says the Lord God. (Am 8:1-3)

Samuel received auditions. His call which we looked at already is an example of an external audition. That is, he heard a voice outside himself. An internal audition is the experience of a voice inside one's head, so to speak. The words are communicated to the mind without any actual hearing by the ears. The prophet knows they are real, nevertheless, and that they come from God. The incident where Samuel anointed David would appear to be of this kind. Jesse presented each of his sons to Samuel, and God indicated to him that none of these was the chosen one, until David was brought in and Samuel was told by God to anoint him.[5]

Despite these experiences, some writers maintain that the prophets were not mystics. Lindblom, for instance, says that the prophets were not mystics, because their conception of God was that God was transcendent and revealed in history. For the prophets, God was always the Other, whereas, he says, the mystics experienced God in the depths of their souls and often had difficulty in conceiving of God as distinct from themselves.[6] I think, however, that he is thinking of only one kind of mysticism. We may regard the prophets as mystics, because they had genuine experiences of God. Their mysticism is very like that of St Teresa of Ávila for whom the relationship with God was always that of 'I and Thou'.

Abraham Heschel has an interesting approach to the prophet's relationship with God. He says that the prophet experiences a 'sympathy with the divine pathos'.[7] The prophet is not just passing on a message, but feels what God feels. The prophet sees things from God's point of view. For instance, the prophet is angry with injustice, because God is angry with injustice. God's anger is an aspect of his love. Although God communicated with the prophets through visions and auditions, this does not rule out the possibility that they also received inspiration through their normal thought processes.

Prophecy in the New Testament

In St Luke's Gospel the ministry of St John the Baptist is introduced in the same way as that of the prophets of the Old Testament. 'The word of God came to John, son of Zechariah in the wilderness' (Lk 3:2). At his birth John had already been hailed as 'the prophet of the Most High'

(Lk 1:76). As an adult, John called people to return to the observance of the covenant. Like Isaiah, his emphasis was on the moral demands of the divine law, on justice and fair dealing. John used the ritual washing of baptism as a way of expressing repentance.

John had the great privilege of baptising Jesus, the one who would baptise with the Holy Spirit. John described himself as 'the voice of one crying out in the wilderness, "Make straight the way of the Lord"' (Jn 1: 23). His mission was to prepare the people for the coming of Jesus. John pointed out Jesus as the Lamb of God and bore witness to the descent of the Holy Spirit on him.

> John testified, 'I saw the Spirit descending from heaven like a dove, and it remained on him. I myself did not know him, but the one who sent me to baptise with water said to me, "He on whom you see the Spirit descend and remain is the one who baptises with the Holy Spirit." And I myself have seen and have testified that this is the Son of God.' (Jn 1:32-34)

During his lifetime Jesus was looked upon as a prophet both by his followers and by the people. When Jesus asks the disciples who people say the Son of Man is, they answer: 'Some say he is John the Baptist, but others Elijah and still others Jeremiah or one of the prophets' (Mt 16:14). The reaction of people to his miracles is to see Jesus as a prophet. When he raises the widow's son to life at Nain, they say: 'A great prophet has risen among us' (Lk 7:16). The disciples on the road to Emmaus express the view that

Jesus of Nazareth 'was a prophet mighty in deed and word before God and all the people' (Lk 24:19).

In the meeting with the Samaritan woman in St John's Gospel the incident opens with Jesus simply being recognised as a Jew and concludes with him being hailed as the Saviour of the World. The woman is gradually coming to a deeper knowledge of who Jesus is. An important point is reached when she says: 'Sir, I see that you are a prophet' (Jn 4:19). The man born blind reaches a similar conclusion. When the Pharisees ask him what he has to say about Jesus, he says: 'He is a prophet' (Jn 9:17).

Jesus, of course, was much more than a prophet. Nevertheless, he was a prophet and he accepted the term. In his sermon in the synagogue in Nazareth, as presented in St Luke's Gospel, Jesus compares himself to the prophets Elijah and Elisha and reminds the congregation that no prophet is accepted in his home town.[8] When he has set out for Jerusalem and the inevitable clash with the authorities which this will entail, Jesus says that it is 'impossible for a prophet to be killed away from Jerusalem.' (Lk 13:33)

Jesus also compares his followers with the prophets:

> Blessed are you when people hate you, and when they exclude you, revile you and defame you on account of the Son of Man. Rejoice on that day and leap for joy, for surely your reward is great in heaven; for that is what their ancestors did to the prophets. (Lk 6:22-23)

Like the prophets, the true disciple will meet with opposition and persecution. The corollary is also true:

> Woe to you when all speak well of you, for this is what their ancestors did to the false prophets. (Lk 6:26)

On the issue of false prophets Jesus also has this to say:

> Beware of false prophets, who come to you in sheep's clothing but inwardly are ravenous wolves. You will know them by their fruits. (Mt 7:15-16)

Prophets are raised up by God. They are often unlikely people and come from unlikely backgrounds. So it is not surprising that there are also people claiming to be prophets who are not. There have always been false prophets as well as true prophets. In the time of Jeremiah, the false prophet Hananiah was telling people what they wanted to hear, whereas Jeremiah was telling it as it was.[9] So it is to be expected that in the history of the Church there would also be false prophets and false mystics.

There is a need for discernment in recognising the true prophet. Jesus himself, in the saying mentioned above tells us that the false prophets would be known by their fruits. Saint Paul tells us that the works of the flesh are: 'fornication, impurity, licentiousness, idolatry, sorcery, enmities, strife, jealousy, anger, quarrels, dissensions, factions, envy, drunkenness, carousing and things like these' (Gal 5:19-21). The false prophet often causes strife and division. A desire for material gain is also an indication that a 'prophet' or 'mystic' is not from God. On the other hand, the fruits of the Holy Spirit are 'love, joy, peace, patience, kindness, generosity, faithfulness, gentleness and self-control' (Gal 5:22). These may be expected to result from the ministry of someone who is truly sent from God. In his discussion on charisms in the First Letter to the Corinthians, St Paul says that those who prophesy speak to other people for their building up and encouragement and consolation.[10]

Generally speaking, it takes time for the work of God to be clearly seen. A very useful principle was enunciated by Gamaliel: that if a spiritual movement is of purely human origin it will fail of its own accord, whereas if it comes from God it will persist and, in fact, it will be indestructible.[11] So caution is needed, particularly in dealing with private revelations. While acknowledging that there are false prophets and false mystics, however, we must remain open to the possibility that there are also true prophets and true mystics.

The Acts of the Apostles tells the story of the Holy Spirit at work in the early Church. As we might expect, it has much to tell us about prophecy. On the day of Pentecost, when the Spirit bestows the gift of tongues on the apostles, Peter interprets the event as fulfilling the words of the Prophet Joel:

> In the last days, it will be, God declares,
> that I will pour out my Spirit upon all flesh,
> and your sons and your daughters shall prophesy,
> and your young men shall see visions,
> and your old men shall dream dreams. (Jl 3:1; Acts 2:17)

Saint Paul

Saint Paul is clearly in the tradition of the prophets. Barnabas and Saul are among those listed as 'prophets and teachers' of the Church at Antioch, before they set out on their first missionary journey.[12] However, much more significant is the whole pattern of Paul's life. He had a rather dramatic call. Like the ancient prophets, Paul was absolutely convinced that his message had been communicated to him directly by God. He spent his life preaching the Word of God and ultimately witnessed to it with his death.

The Acts of the Apostles introduces us to Paul or Saul, to give him his Jewish name, as a persecutor of the Christians. He was present at the stoning of Stephen. After this he went from house to house arresting followers of the Way and sending them to prison.[13] Some of the Jerusalem Christians must have fled to Damascus, because that was where Saul went next with letters from the high priest to arrest the followers of Jesus and have them brought back to Jerusalem. Why Saul was so opposed to this new sect is not clear. I suspect that his opposition stemmed from fear. Perhaps in some corner of his mind it had occurred to him that maybe Jesus really was the Messiah. This would undermine his whole religious mindset, which was based on the scrupulous observance of the Law of Moses, together with the oral traditions which the Pharisees had added on to it. Jesus had revised the Law of Moses on his own authority and he had been quite dismissive about the traditions of the Pharisees.

A short distance outside Damascus, Saul was confronted by Jesus himself in a blinding vision of light. He heard a voice asking him: 'Saul, Saul, why do you persecute me?' He asked: 'Who are you Lord?' The reply was: 'I am Jesus whom you persecute' (Acts 9:3-5). This was a shattering experience for Saul. He had to be led into Damascus and spent a few days in a state of shock, until he was visited by Ananias who restored his sight and baptised him. To give Saul his due, when he was shown that he had got it wrong, he accepted that and for the rest of his life devoted his considerable energy to the cause of Jesus.

The lessons of that first encounter stayed with Paul. Firstly, Jesus was supposed to be dead, but was in fact alive. The resurrection of Jesus became the kernel of Paul's message and the cornerstone of his theology. The second lesson was that Jesus identifies with his followers: 'Why are you persecuting me?' Paul's theology of the Church as the Body of Christ comes from this experience. Thirdly, Paul himself had been chosen personally by Jesus and his life had been turned upside down. He could not but tell others about this. His conversion was also his call to be an apostle.[14]

In his life as a Pharisee, before his encounter with Jesus, Paul had carefully constructed an edifice of perfection by the observance of the Law. This all came apart on the road to Damascus. Now he realised that salvation was to be found in Christ, not through our own efforts at keeping the Law. Paul could see that the cultural aspects of the Jewish Law, such as circumcision and the dietary regulations, were no longer relevant or important. As a follower of Christ he did not have much patience with those who could not see that quite so clearly. Some of the senior figures in the early Church were not very happy with the way in which he pushed out the boundaries.

Saint Paul became the great missionary, not just in terms of the distances he travelled, but in terms of what we would now call inculturation. He was able to see what was essential to the Christian message and what was cultural wrapping. The essential message had to be preserved and proclaimed, but the cultural wrapping could be left behind and new forms of expression found. The same challenge faces missionaries in every age.

Prophecy in the Life of the Church

The Hebrew prophets received revelation from God and communicated it to the community. Christ, as the Word made flesh, is the fullness of divine revelation. What role is there for the prophet now that God has spoken his final word in his Son? There are three senses in which we may speak of prophets in the life of the Church. Firstly, all the baptised and confirmed have been anointed by the Holy Spirit and share in Christ's anointing as priest, prophet and king.[15] All Christians are entrusted with the mission of the Church to proclaim Christ to the world.[16] Secondly, there are people in the Church whom God raises up to remind us of particular gospel values which are being ignored or neglected. These people are not telling us anything new, but they are witnesses and we may speak of people in the Church who give a prophetic witness. In the same way the Hebrew prophets did not always have something new to communicate. Most of the time, they were reminding people of their obligations to the Mosaic Covenant. Thirdly, there are people who have mystical experiences and receive 'private revelations'. These private revelations do not add to divine revelation, but again remind us of some aspect of it that is particularly relevant to the time. These are prophets and mystics.

The psychological experiences of the mystics seem to have been very similar to those of the prophets in the Bible.

Many of them were founders of local Churches or religious communities. Examples would be St Patrick, St Francis of Assisi, St Ignatius of Loyola and St Teresa of Ávila. Others like St Catherine of Siena, St Margaret Mary Alacoque and St Bernadette of Lourdes influenced the life of the Church. Saint Catherine advised the pope to return to Rome. Saint Margaret Mary spread the message of God's love revealed in the Sacred Heart of Jesus.

There have been many men and women in the history of the Church who did not have unusual psychological experiences or receive any special messages, but who may be regarded as prophets because their lives proclaimed a message from God. The Holy Spirit was working through their normal thought processes and emotions. All those who possessed the charism of preaching and the gift of teaching can be seen in this way. Those who spoke out against injustice are particularly in the tradition of the ancient prophets. Doctor Martin Luther King Junior and Archbishop Oscar Romero are two examples from the last century.

Many examples could be given of prophets in the history of the Church. The Holy Spirit constantly raises up particular individuals to bear witness to the message of Jesus Christ. This could be the subject of a whole book, or rather a series of books. In what follows, I give just a few examples in order to illustrate the point.

Saint Francis of Assisi

In the thirteenth century Europe experienced an evangelical awakening. A number of new religious groups came on the scene, inspired by the idea of living according to the

Gospel. The most original of these groups was that of the Franciscans. It was inspired by the charismatic figure of Francis of Assisi (1182–1226). Francis was the son of a wealthy merchant and dreamt of winning fame and glory as a soldier. He was taken prisoner during a battle in the ongoing feud between Assisi and Perugia and spent over a year in an unsanitary dungeon. Some time after coming home he became seriously ill and mentally troubled. This was a life-changing experience for him. When Francis recovered he was searching for a new purpose in life.

As we have seen, all the prophets experienced a turning point in their lives which usually took the form of a call. One day, in the spring of 1206, Francis wandered into the half-ruined church of San Damiano on the outskirts of Assisi and, as he contemplated the face of Christ on the icon crucifix over the altar, he heard a voice saying to him: 'Francis, don't you see that my house has collapsed? Go and repair it for me.'[17] That Christ had spoken to him personally filled Francis with great joy. He presumed that the Lord was referring to the actual church of San Damiano and set about repairing it. It would become clear later that the words had a deeper meaning.

After this incident, Francis started to live a simple life, spending much time in prayer and occupying himself with the physical labour of rebuilding San Damiano. His abandonment of his previous lifestyle as a well-to-do man about town attracted attention, most of it unfavourable. However, some of his friends realised that this new life was not a fad, but something genuine, and also that it had made Francis extremely happy. Two of them, Bernardo di Quintavalle and Pietro di Catanio, decided to join him.

Both gave up wealth and successful careers in order to do so.

With his two new companions, Francis decided that what they needed to do was to go to the church and see what instructions Christ gave his disciples. They went into the church of St Nicholas in Assisi and Francis opened the missal on the altar in three places. The three Gospel passages which he found were:

> If you wish to be perfect, go, sell what you have and give it to the poor, and you shall have treasure in heaven. (Mt 19:21)
> Take nothing for the journey. (Lk 9:3)
> If any man will come after me, let him deny himself. (Mt 16:24)

Immediately, the three companions decided to live according to these texts.[18]

Francis and his companions were soon joined by others. As the movement began to grow, Francis realised that they would need the approval of the pope. Many of the evangelical groups that had sprung up during this period were very critical of the hierarchy and ended up outside the Church. Francis, however, always had great respect for bishops and clergy, because, even if they were unworthy, their authority came from God. He had already received the blessing of Bishop Guido of Assisi. In 1209 Francis and his companions set out for Rome to have their way of life approved by Pope Innocent III.

When the little group from Assisi arrived in Rome, they were dressed like beggars and must have looked very strange to the members of the papal court. In fact, many of the cardinals were not impressed and thought that the proposed way of life was too extreme. However, after some days, Pope Innocent received the group. To the surprise of many he gave them his blessing and permission to preach penitence. Innocent may have been influenced in his decision by a dream he is said to have had in which the Lateran Basilica, symbol of the Universal Church, was seen to be falling down. A poor little man came and propped it up. The poor little man was Francis. Francis promised obedience to the pope and the other brothers promised obedience to Francis. Before leaving Rome, Francis was ordained a deacon.[19] The new order was given more formal approval later by Innocent's successor, Pope Honorius III, who approved the Rule of the Friars Minor in 1223.[20]

The group of 'penitents' from Assisi now became the Order of Friars Minor. The new order grew rapidly. Together with St Clare, St Francis founded a second order for women, the Poor Clares. He also founded a third order for lay people, who wanted to follow his way of life while continuing with their secular occupations and family commitments. The Third Order of St Francis is now called the Secular Franciscan Order. A number of other religious orders followed this way of enabling lay people to share in their spirituality.

Saint Francis had a great sense of the reality of the Incarnation. God really did become a human being and share our life. Saint Francis popularised the Christmas crib and on one occasion organised a living crib for Christmas in Assisi. The Stations of the Cross, a devotion developed later by the Franciscans, was very much in keeping with his spirituality. He spent long hours contemplating the Passion of Christ, and towards the end of his life, received the *Stigmata*, the marks of Christ's wounds on his body.

Saint Francis had great reverence for creation. He rejoiced in the beauty that God had created. Many stories about his life relate to his compassion for wild creatures, such as his taming of the wolf of Gubbio and his preaching to the birds. His Canticle of the Creatures expresses this aspect of his spirituality. This tied in with his emphasis on poverty. For him the good things that God gives us are to be appreciated and shared, not possessed. Saint Francis was also a peacemaker. Not only did he bring about reconciliation between feuding factions on a number of occasions in Italy, he also travelled to Egypt during the Fifth Crusade and tried to make peace between Christians and Muslims.

Saint Francis was a prophetic figure to the Church in his time. He reminded people of the humanity of Christ and of the Gospel values of peace, simplicity and joy. He was canonised by Pope Gregory IX in 1227.[21]

Saint Bernadette

Bernadette Soubirous[22] was born in Lourdes in 1844. Between February 11 and 16 July 1858 Bernadette experienced eighteen apparitions of the Blessed Virgin Mary at the Grotto of Massabielle near Lourdes. Bernadette was fourteen years old at the time. Her family had fallen on hard times. She lacked education, as she had missed school because of ill health and because, as the eldest, she had to help mind her younger brothers and sisters while her mother went out to work. Bernadette had not yet made her First Holy Communion.

When Bernadette first saw the vision of a beautiful Lady, her first reaction was to make the Sign of the Cross. She then said the Rosary, as she was to do on each occasion when she visited the Grotto. The Lady asked Bernadette to come to the Grotto for fifteen days. During this time people heard about the apparitions and large crowds started to come to see what was happening. The Lady asked Bernadette to do penance and to pray for sinners. She showed her a spring of water coming out of the rock and told her to drink the water and wash in it.[23]

Towards the end of the fifteen days the Lady asked Bernadette to go to the priests and tell them that she wanted a chapel built and to have the people come in procession. This was a rather daunting task for a young girl. The parish priest, Fr Peyramale, was a rather austere man and he was not inclined to believe her. However, Bernadette delivered her message and stuck to her story. She was also interrogated by the police and by the local magistrate and examined by a doctor. She calmly recounted her experiences without exaggeration, but without denying what she has seen and been told. For instance, she did not claim to have seen the Blessed Virgin, but a Lady. The parish priest told her to ask the Lady her name. It was another two weeks before the Lady gave the answer to that question. On 25 March the Lady said that she was the Immaculate Conception. This convinced Fr Peyramale and that evening he wrote to the Bishop, Msgr Laurence, who later formally recognised the authenticity of the apparitions. When he met Bernadette he was impressed by her sincerity and her good sense. The authenticity of the message given to Bernadette has been proven by her own integrity and by the fruits that have resulted from the shrine of Lourdes.[24]

After the apparitions, Bernadette became a boarder in the hospice run by the Sisters of Charity of Nevers in Lourdes. Here she was able to continue her education and was protected from journalists and others who wanted to hear her story. She felt called to join the sisters and in 1866 she left Lourdes for the motherhouse of the congregation in Nevers. There she led a life of prayer and of caring for the sick. Her life reflected what was happening in Lourdes, which had become a great centre of prayer and of ministry to the sick. Bernadette's health had never been good and for the last period of her life she became a permanent invalid. She died on 16 April 1897. Her body was exhumed in 1909 and found to be intact. After Bernadette was declared Blessed in 1925, her body was placed in a shrine in the convent chapel in Nevers. Saint Bernadette was canonised by Pope Pius XI on 8 December 1933.[25] She was not declared a saint because she had seen Our Lady, but because she had been faithful to the mission that had been entrusted to her. Her whole life bore witness to the message of prayer, compassion and penance of which Lourdes became the sign.

Saint Bernadette was faithful in passing on the message she received and so was instrumental in establishing Lourdes as a great centre of pilgrimage. Through this simple act she was a prophet. The nineteenth century was a time when the Christian religion was being undermined by rationalism and atheism. God used a young girl, who was without education but who had faith, to point people in the right direction, to show them that the heart of religion was love, expressed in devotion to God and service of our neighbour.

Saint John XXIII

Angelo Roncalli was born near Bergamo, Italy, in 1881. He was ordained to the priesthood in 1904. He worked for some time as secretary to the Bishop of Bergamo and also taught in the Roman Seminary. He spent most of his ministry as a papal envoy in Bulgaria, Turkey and France, until he was made Patriarch of Venice in 1953.

Angelo was elected pope in 1958 and took the name John XXIII. As he was elderly and unassuming, some commentators at the time thought that he would be an interim figure and would merely keep the seat warm until a more dynamic successor came along. However, St John made an immediate impact. People of all creeds and none responded to his warm and simple manner.

Saint John changed the history of the Catholic Church by calling the Second Vatican Council. The inspiration to hold the Council came to St John unexpectedly in a manner similar to the way in which the Word of God came to the ancient prophets. In his opening speech to the Council he explained how this came about.

> As regards the initiative for the great event which gathers us here, it will suffice to repeat as historical documentation our personal account of the first sudden bringing up in our heart and lips of the simple words, 'Ecumenical Council'. We uttered these words in the presence of the Sacred College of Cardinals on that memorable 25 January 1959, the feast of the Conversion of St Paul, in the basilica dedicated to him. It was completely unexpected, like a flash of heavenly light, shedding sweetness in eyes and hearts.[26]

The pope seemed to have been as surprised as anyone else about this announcement, but he was convinced that it came about as a result of an inspiration of the Holy Spirit. It was an example of the prophetic charism at work. This was confirmed by the fact that the announcement gave rise to great fervour throughout the world in expectation of the Council.

Saint John went on to explain to the assembled bishops that this was going to be a different kind of council. Its purpose was to enable the Church to face the future without fear. The two great themes of John's pontificate were *aggiornamento* and *convivienza*. It is hard to find exact English equivalents for these terms. *Aggiornamento* means updating or renewal. Saint John believed that the Church needed to address itself to the modern world in today's language. As he said: 'The substance of the ancient doctrine of the deposit of faith is one thing, and the way in which it is presented is another.'[27] The latter should be reformulated in a way which would be pastorally effective.

Convivienza means living with others or cooperation. Saint John realised that the world was coming together in a new way. Catholics needed to form positive relationships with other Christians, with people of other faiths and with the secular world. John's vision was truly prophetic. He saw that the world was on the cusp of a new age and he encouraged the Church to prepare for the future in a positive spirit, with confidence and trust in God. Above all, he believed that God's loving plan of salvation was unfolding despite the negative elements that might suggest otherwise. He told the newly assembled Council:

> We feel we must disagree with those prophets of gloom, who are always forecasting disaster, as though the end of the world were at hand. In the present order of things, divine providence is leading us to a new order of human relations which, by men's own efforts and even beyond their very expectations, are directed towards the fulfilment of God's superior and inscrutable designs.[28]

Over the next three years, from October 1962 to December 1965, the Second Vatican Council was to work out the agenda for the Church for the rest of the twentieth century and beyond. Saint John XXIII died on 3 June 1963, but the work he had begun was continued by his successor Blessed Paul VI. The Council completely transformed relationships at many levels, within the Catholic Church, with other Christians and with the wider world. The contribution of St John XXIII himself to this transformation cannot be overestimated. A love for other people radiated from him. In particular the relationship with other Christians and with the Jews is worth noting.

Before St John XXIII became pope, relations between the Catholic Church and other Christian Churches had been at best polite and distant, while at times it had been hostile and polemical. Catholics were not altogether to blame for this situation. All the Churches had contributed to it. The Protestant Churches, however, had begun to come together since 1910 with the Missionary Conference in Edinburgh which is regarded as the beginning of the Ecumenical Movement. The World Council of Churches was founded in 1948. The Orthodox Patriarchate of Constantinople was involved from the beginning. Apart from some work behind the scenes by individuals like Dom Lambert Beauduin and Cardinal Mercier in Belgium, the Catholic Church remained aloof from these developments. However, the election of St John completely transformed the atmosphere. In 1960 he set up the Secretariat for Promoting Christian Unity and when the Second Vatican Council opened in 1962, Ecumenism was one of the major items on the agenda. 'John XXIII, Bishop of Rome' is included in the calendar of the Lutheran Church in America in their *Lutheran Book of Worship* (2005) under 3 June. He is the only pope of the second millennium to be commemorated.

Saint John's last encyclical was *Pacem in Terris* which was published on 11 April 1963, two months before his death on 3 June of that year. This encyclical was addressed not just to Catholics or Christians, but to all people of good will. It was Saint John's final prophetic word on how society and the world should be. He said that war was no longer a way for humanity to resolve conflict. Peace will come about if there is justice, which means respecting the human rights of each and every person. At the basis of this is the dignity of the human person. Forty years later, in his message for World Peace Day, St John Paul II summed up John's vision: 'With the profound intuition that was characteristic of him, John XXIII identified the essential conditions for peace in four requirements of the human spirit: truth, justice, love and freedom.'[29]

Saint John was beatified by Saint John Paul II on 3 September 2000 and was canonised by Pope Francis on 27 April 2014 along with St John Paul II.

Chiara Lubich

Chiara Lubich was the founder of the Focolare Movement. She was born in Trent, Italy, on 22 January 1920, the second of four children. Her baptismal name was Silvia. She took the name Chiara on becoming a member of the Franciscan Third Order in her early twenties. On leaving school Chiara qualified as an elementary school teacher.[30]

The Focolare Movement began in 1943 in Trent where Chiara was sharing an apartment with three other girls, all of whom were committed to living the Christian life in a radical way. They knew that meant a life of love. Jesus said that there was no greater love than to lay down one's life for one's friend. This is what the girls were prepared to do. Like St Francis of Assisi, Chiara and her companions were guided by the Word of God. They took a word of Scripture, a sentence from the Gospel, and put it into practice. This became a basic feature of the spirituality of the movement. It is called the Word of Life. An early example was 'Give and gifts will be given to you' (Lk 6:38). Times were tough, as this was during the Second World War. They had very little food, but when a poor man came asking for food, the girls gave him what they had. Next day they received a gift of food. The Scripture was literally true. They came to have great trust in divine providence. A saying of Jesus that was to be foundational for the spirituality of the Focolare Movement was, 'Where two or three are gathered together in my name, there am I in the midst of them' (Mt 18:20). If we are united, Jesus is with us and then everything is possible.[31]

By 1945 around five hundred people already shared in the ideal of the young women. The movement continued to grow. In 1962 it was formally approved by the Catholic Church under the official name of the Work of Mary. Around this time the movement also got involved in ecumenical dialogue. In 1967 Chiara met Patriarch Athenagoras I of Constantinople for the first time. He considered himself a focolarino. Also in 1967 Chiara founded New Families, a movement within the Focolare Movement.[32]

Since the early days in Trent, there had been summer gatherings in the nearby mountains. Mariapolis, 'City of Mary', was the name given to these gatherings. It was a new kind of retreat and at the same time a kind of holiday. It provided an opportunity to live the spirituality together in a more intense way. The Mariapolis is still an annual event and now takes place in many countries. It is about living the commandment of Jesus: 'Love one another as I have loved you' (Jn 15:12). One of the attractive things about the movement is that it is very practical.

In 1964 the opportunity came about to set up a permanent Mariapolis at Loppiano in Italy. Since then a number of small towns with a similar inspiration have been set up in various parts of the world. These are centres where it can be demonstrated that the spirituality of unity can be lived in all aspects of life: family, education, business, sport and the arts. In 1991 Chiara launched the Economy of Communion, a project designed to show that business could be run on Christian principles.[33]

Focolare means 'hearth' in Italian. Chiara herself was like a fire to which people came for warmth. She had a profound insight into Our Lord's Prayer in John 17 that all may be on. The unity for which Jesus prayed comes from the Trinity. The Persons of the Trinity live in each other. Jesus speaks of being in the Father and the Father being in him. The Son glorifies the Father and the Father glorifies the Son. In a way that is derived from the unity of the Trinity, the spirituality of unity involves seeking the good of the other person and promoting the holiness of the other person. It is a spirituality of communion.

The source of unity is Jesus himself. In the Incarnation God made himself one with us. The ultimate point of identification with us was the Passion of Jesus. The moment in the Passion where Jesus suffered most was when he cried out: 'My God, my God, why have you forsaken me?' (Mt 27: 46). At that moment in his human nature Jesus experienced the anguish of man's distance from God. Paradoxically, it was in that moment that God was nearest to suffering humanity. For this reason Chiara saw in 'Jesus Forsaken' the cornerstone of unity.

Chiara placed great trust in the wisdom of the Church and in the guidance given to the Hierarchy by the Holy Spirit. The encouragement which she received from the popes was very important to her. Saint John XXIII approved the movement in 1962. Blessed Paul VI received Chiara in audience a number of times and encouraged the work of the new movement. Saint John Paul II invited Chiara to attend the Synod of Bishops on a number of occasions. At the Pentecost Vigil held in St Peter's Square in 1998, she addressed the gathering of ecclesial movements. Also around this time the movement got involved in interreligious dialogue.[34]

Chiara Lubich was a prophetic figure because she opened up a new approach to spirituality. There are many parallels between Chiara and St Teresa of Ávila. Both were given extraordinary graces to found new movements in the Church of their day. Both were cultured, charming and cheerful. They were people of deep spirituality. Both Teresa and Chiara left a wealth of writing to the Church. In her book *The Interior Castle*, Teresa describes finding God present in the depths of one's soul. Chiara refers to this and says that what we have to do today is to construct the Exterior Castle.[35] In other words, we have to find God in each other and build a Christian community. The insights of St Teresa and of Chiara complement one another. Chiara Lubich died on 14 March 2008. The cause for her beatification was introduced on 7 December 2013.[36]

Prophetic Figures in the Irish Church

There have been many prophetic figures in the history of the Irish Church. Saint Patrick stands out as a man sent by God to preach the Gospel. He experienced a number of dreams in which he was given instructions about his life. Like St Paul, Patrick was convinced that his call to be a missionary came to him directly from God.

The writers of the lives of the Irish saints during the early period (i.e. before the twelfth century) seem to have taken it for granted that any saint worthy of the name would have the gift of prophecy. This is true of both men and women. For instance, in the *Life of St Darerca* we read, 'Among other graces of the Holy Spirit, the spirit of prophecy shone in her soul.'[37] It was believed that the druids had the ability to predict the future.[38] So their Christian rivals had to be at least as good as them. It is probably for this reason that these writers saw prophecy mainly in terms of predicting the future, but the saints they depicted were usually rather strong characters whose lives also made a prophetic statement. Saint Colmcille and St Malachy are credited with more extensive prophecies. Other figures who fit into the prophetic mould are the martyrs of the sixteenth and seventeenth centuries. This group includes men and women, lay people and clerics.

Nano Nagle

Hanora Nagle, who was always known as Nano, was born in 1718 to a well-to-do family of Anglo-Norman ancestry in Ballygriffin, Co. Cork. Nano grew up in that pleasant countryside and in a devout Catholic family. In her teens she was sent to Paris to further her education and also because Irish Catholics who could afford it tended to go to France in order to have a better life. At the time life for Catholics in Ireland was restricted by the Penal Laws. Nano was joined in Paris by her sister Ann and stayed there until the death of her father, Garret Nagle, in 1746.[39]

This was the France of Louis XV and, as a young person, Nano was not above engaging in frivolity. She went to parties and balls. On one occasion she was coming back from a ball in the small hours of the morning and she noticed a group of poor people waiting outside a church. Nano's awareness of her vocation to help the poor came about gradually, but it may have begun with this incident which made a deep impression on her. When their father died, Nano and Ann returned to Ireland and went to live with their mother in Bachelor's Quay in Dublin. They were to live there for three or four years. Another incident during this period shows that Nano was becoming aware of the needs of the poor. She had brought back a length of silk from Paris with the intention of getting a dressmaker to make it into a gown. When she got around to doing so she discovered that Ann had sold it and used the proceeds to distribute food to the poor.

Mrs Nagle died in 1748 and a year or so later Ann died. Nano went back to Ballygriffin, but could not settle. She returned to Paris with the intention of becoming a nun in an enclosed convent. With the help of a Jesuit spiritual director, Nano soon realised that this was not God's will for her. She returned to Ireland and went to live with her brother Joseph and his wife in Cork City.[40] Nano soon began to help the poor and the sick and in 1755 she opened a school for thirty poor girls in a mud cabin in Cove Lane. By 1769 she had seven schools in Cork, five for girls and two for boys. The children were taught reading, writing and arithmetic. The girls also learned domestic skills, such as sewing. Nano employed some teachers with money which she received from her uncle Joseph Nagle. She taught religion herself, going around all seven schools to do so. Her greatest joy was preparing children for First Confession and First Holy Communion. She spent the time after school visiting the poor and the sick all over the city. As well as this, Nano spent long hours in prayer. One of her devotions was reading the Passion of Our Lord.

Nano worried about what would happen to her schools after her death. She came to the conclusion that the best way of ensuring the continuation of her work was to entrust it to a community of religious. Nano arranged to have the Ursuline Sisters in Paris make a foundation in Cork. Some young Irish women had recently joined the Ursuline Order and these were to be the core of the new community in

Cork. They took up residence in the convent which Nano provided for them in 1771.[41] The Ursulines later moved to another site and this convent became the South Presentation Convent. The Ursulines made an important contribution to Catholic education in Ireland. From this beginning in Cork, they were later to make foundations in Waterford, Thurles and Sligo. However, it soon became evident that they were not really the answer to Nano's problem, which was the continuation of her apostolate to the very poor. The Ursulines were hampered by their constitutions which included the rule of enclosure. Their apostolate had to be conducted within the walls of the convent and so they could not visit the poor or go out to teach in the little cabin schools.

Nano had great trust in divine providence. She used to say, 'The Almighty is All-sufficient'. After some hesitation, Nano came up with a new plan. In 1775 she founded the Sisters of Charitable Instruction of the Sacred Heart of Jesus. She already had a number of women who taught in her schools as volunteers. Nano chose two of these and invited them to join her as postulants in the new congregation. These were Mary Fouhy and Elizabeth Bourke, both natives of Cork. They were joined by a fourth before the year was out: Mary Ann Collins, also a native of Cork, who would become Nano's successor. All four pronounced simple vows in the presence of the Bishop of Cork, Dr John Butler, on 24 June 1777.[42]

Nano Nagle died on 26 April 1784, at the age of sixty-five. By then her work was firmly established in Cork. One of her great friends was Dr Francis Moylan. He had been her parish priest when she founded the new congregation.

At first he had advised against the move, but when Nano persuaded him of its necessity, he gave her his full support. In the same year, 1775, he was made Bishop of Kerry. In 1787 Dr Moylan returned to his native city as Bishop of Cork. After Nano's death he was anxious to make sure that her congregation would have proper canonical approval. This required the drawing up of constitutions. He was in a unique position to have this work done as he knew exactly what Nano's wishes were. In 1790 he sent the Constitutions of the Sisters of Charitable Instruction to the Holy See for approval. Pope Pius VI gave his approval the following year. In 1793 the sisters adopted new constitutions and a new name, the Sisters of the Presentation of the Blessed Virgin Mary.[43]

By 1800 there were six foundations. Two were in Cork – the South Presentation and the North Presentation. The others were in Killarney, Dublin, Waterford and Kilkenny. In the decades that followed the movement begun by Nano Nagle grew and spread. Communities of Presentation Sisters were established in cities and towns all over Ireland. Subsequently the Presentation Sisters spread further afield and are currently ministering in Britain, Canada, the United States, Australia, New Zealand, India, Pakistan and the Philippines.[44] In 2013 Nano Nagle was declared Venerable by Pope Francis. She was a truly heroic woman who pioneered the apostolate of bringing education to the poor in Ireland. Her life and her legacy are prophetic signs of God's love.

As well as founding the Presentation Sisters, Nano also influenced the foundation and growth of other congregations dedicated to education and helping the poor. In 1798 the

Presentation Sisters came to Waterford. This inspired Blessed Edmund Rice to do for boys what the sisters were doing for girls. He opened his first school in 1802. In 1808 he and his associates became religious brothers. At first they copied the constitutions of the sisters, but later adopted a different rule. This gave rise to the Christian Brothers and the Presentation Brothers.[45]

Catherine McCauley founded the Sisters of Mercy in Baggot Street, Dublin, in 1831. She did her noviciate with the Presentation Sisters, but founded her own congregation as she wanted her sisters to be able to visit the poor in their homes, something that Nano had always done herself.[46] The Mercy Sisters are engaged in nursing as well as teaching. Mary Aikenhead, foundress of the Irish Sisters of Charity, was also influenced by the ideals of Nano Nagle. She grew up in Cork and was received into the Catholic Church by Nano's friend Bishop Moylan. The Sisters of Charity initially took care of orphans and then took on nursing and social work. They got involved in education in 1830.[47]

In the twentieth century the prophetic figures were the missionaries, people like Mother Mary Martin and Fr Rufus Halley who were discussed in Chapter Two. There were literally hundreds of others from all over Ireland and they went all over the world. Another person who stands out in the twentieth century is Frank Duff.

Frank Duff

Frank Duff[48] was a man ahead of his time in his understanding of the apostolate of the laity. Frank was born in Dublin in 1889. When he left school, he worked in the Civil Service. In 1913 Frank joined the Society of St

Vincent de Paul. There was appalling poverty in Dublin at this time and the members of the society tried to alleviate it. Frank became aware that there was also a spiritual poverty that needed to be addressed. In 1916 he wrote a pamphlet entitled *Can we be Saints?* in which he expressed the conviction that all Christians are called to be saints. This was the first of many pamphlets and perhaps the first indication that he was a man ahead of his time. The idea of the universal call to holiness was proclaimed at Vatican II, but in 1916 many spiritual writers held the view that only religious were called to 'perfection' and that it was enough for the laity to 'save their souls'.

In 1921 Frank Duff founded the Legion of Mary as a lay apostolic organisation at the service of the Church. It had the two-fold purpose of the sanctification of its members and the spread of Christ's Kingdom on earth through Our Lady. Frank borrowed many ideas from the Society of St Vincent de Paul, such as the weekly meeting and the practice of sending the members out in pairs to do visitation. The Legionaries, however, would not give alms as this would interfere with their apostolate which was to evangelise. The spirituality of the Legion is based on the writings of St Louis Marie de Montfort, especially *True Devotion to the Blessed Virgin Mary* which had greatly influenced Frank when he first read it in 1917. Frank's civil service background gave him a very systematic and organised approach.

In 1932 the International Eucharistic Congress was held in Dublin. By this time the Legion had grown considerably in Ireland. The Congress gave the Legionaries the opportunity to showcase the new organisation to bishops, priests and missionaries from all over the world. As a result the Legion was established in many countries and became particularly important on the missions as a way of organising the laity. As we have seen, it played a particularly significant role in the Columban mission to China.

Frank took other initiatives as well. He set up the Pauline Circle as a forum for dialogue with Protestants. Again he was ahead of his time, or in this case ahead of the Archbishop who thought the idea was too *avant-garde* and had it brought to an end. A more successful idea was *Peregrinatio pro Christo* which is a project whereby Legionaries can go abroad for short periods to do apostolic work.

In 1965 Frank Duff was invited to attend the fourth session of the Second Vatican Council. Frank had in fact anticipated the teaching of the Council that lay people could be apostles in their own right and not just as assisting in the apostolate of bishops and priests. By the end of the twentieth century the Legion of Mary had over three million active members spread throughout the world.

Frank Duff died on 7 November 1980. The cause for his beatification was introduced in 1996.

NOTES

1. E.g. 1 Kings 21:17–29.
2. Cf. J. Lindblom, *Prophecy in Ancient Israel* (Oxford: Basil Blackwell, 1973), p. 108.
3. Cf. Gerhard von Rad, *The Message of the Prophets* (New York: HarperCollins, 1967), p. 39.
4. Cf. 2 Kings 8:11.
5. 1 Samuel 16:4–13.
6. Cf. Lindblom, op. cit., pp. 299 ff.
7. Abraham J. Heschel, *The Prophets* (New York: Harper Perennial Classics, 2001), p. 31.
8. Luke 4:24-27.

9. Cf. Jeremiah 26.
10. 1 Corinthians 14:3.
11. Cf. Acts 5: 38-39.
12. Cf. Acts 13:1.
13. Cf. Acts 7:55–8:3.
14. Cf. Michael Mullins, *The Acts of the Apostles A Commentary* (Dublin: Columba Press, 2013), pp. 108–9.
15. Cf. the prayer that accompanies the anointing with Chrism in the Rite of Baptism.
16. 'The holy People of God shares also in Christ's prophetic office', *Lumen Gentium 12*.
17. Adrian House, *Francis of Assisi* (London: Pimlico, 2001), p. 64.
18. Cf. House, op. cit., pp. 78–9.
19. Cf. House, op. cit., pp. 93–9.
20. Cf. House, op. cit., p. 299.
21. Cf. House, op. cit., p. 287.
22. Cf. Antonio Bernardo, *Bernadette raconte ses apparitions* (Lourdes: André Doucet et Fils, 1995).
23. Cf. Mgr Jacques Perrier, '50 Questions about Lourdes', *Lourdes Magazine* (April–May, 2010), pp. 30–3.
24. Ibid.
25. Cf. 'Bernadette Messenger of Heaven', *Lourdes Magazine* (Special Edition, 2008); 'Canonisation of Bernadette, The Dossier', *Lourdes Magazine* (April–May, 2009).
26. Saint John's Opening Speech to the Council in Walter M. Abbott SJ, *The Documents of Vatican II* (London: Geoffrey Chapman, 1967), pp. 711–2.
27. Ibid., p. 715.
28. Ibid., p. 712.
29. Pope John Paul II, Message for World Peace Day, 1 January 2003.
30. Cf. Michele Zanzucchi, 'Chiara, Her Story from Trent to the World', *Living City*, Special Issue, vol. 47, no. 5/6, p. 4.
31. Cf. Zanzucchi, op. cit., pp. 4–7.
32. Cf. Zanzucchi, op. cit., pp. 7–11.
33. Cf. Zanzucchi, op. cit., pp. 10–13.
34. Cf. Zanzucchi, op. cit., pp. 11–14.

35. Chiara Lubich, *A New Way The Spirituality of Unity* (London: New City, 2006), p. 35.
36. Living City (January 2014), vol. 53, no. 1, p. 5.
37. 'The Life of St Darerca, or Moninna, the Abbess in Liam de Paor', *St Patrick's World* (Dublin,: Four Courts Press, 1993), p. 284.
38. Cf. Louis Gougaud, *Christianity in Celtic Lands* (Dublin: Four Courts Press, 1992), p. 16.
39. Cf. Sr Mary Pius O'Farrell, *Nano Nagle Woman of the Gospel* (Cork: Cork Publishing Company, 1996), pp. 53–61.
40. Cf. O'Farrell, op. cit., pp. 66–7.
41. Cf. O'Farrell, op. cit., pp. 103–43.
42. Cf. O'Farrell, op. cit., pp. 146–9.
43. Cf. O'Farrell, op. cit., pp. 204–12. Ironically the constitutions of 1793 included enclosure, contrary to the wishes of both Nano Nagle and Bishop Moylan, but by then the work of the sisters was well established and the poor came to them.
44. Cf. Mary Ryan D'Arcy, *The Saints of Ireland* (Cork: Mercier Press, 1974), p. 213.
45. Cf. O'Farrell, op. cit., pp. 273–6.
46. Cf. O'Farrell, op. cit., pp. 284–7.
47. Cf. O'Farrell, op. cit., p. 279.
48. Cf. Frank Duff, *A Memoir* (London: CTS, 1981); Boniface Hanley OFM, *Frank Duff, One of the Best* (Dublin: Praedicanda Publications).

CHAPTER FIVE

SAINT JOHN'S SPIRITUALITY OF THE INCARNATION

'In the Beginning was the Word'

Saint John's Gospel begins with the idea of the Word. The Word was with God in the beginning. What God was, the Word was (Jn 1:1). Why does John use this concept of the Word to express the relationship between God the Father and his Son? Language is what makes communication between persons possible. If I have a thought in my mind, the only way I can share that with you is through language, through the word. A word is the expression of a person. It begins in the heart as a sentiment or idea. It is formulated in the mind and expressed in speech. To say that the Son is the Word of the Father is to say that the Son is the most intimate expression of what the Father is.

The word is what makes us human. It makes the sharing of ideas possible. It creates community. What makes the revelation to the people of Israel unique is that God spoke. God is revealed in nature as powerful, wise and beautiful, but it is only through his Word that God is revealed as personal. Through his Word God invites us into a relationship with him. This communication of God with us reached its climax when 'the Word became flesh and lived among us' (Jn 1:14). The Incarnation is the key concept in St John's Gospel and in the Epistles of John. It provides a fruitful starting point for a distinctive spirituality which we may call 'Johannine'.

Word Made Flesh: The Incarnation

The word 'flesh', *sarx* in Greek, expresses all that is fragile about the human condition. The flesh is born, lives and dies. It is subject to the ravages of time. It experiences sickness, pain and hunger. It is prone to sin. The flesh is weak. Yet it is this frail flesh that God the Word becomes. So this is the mystery of the human life of Jesus. The First Epistle of John is in awe at the tangibility of the incarnate God: 'what we have heard, what we have seen with our eyes, what we have looked at and touched with our hands' (1 Jn 1:1).

The flesh experiences the joy and sorrow of being human. If Jesus had been a twentieth-century Jew, he would probably have died in Auschwitz. As a first-century Jew, Jesus was crucified. This was the most cruel and humiliating way to die at that time. The death penalty was not uncommon at the time. Crucifixion was the way in which the Romans executed slaves and others who did not have the status of being Roman citizens. When the slaves' rebellion led by Spartacus was crushed in 71 BC, crosses lined the road from Rome to Capua with the thousands who were crucified.

Jesus could have avoided the Cross. He says: 'I lay my life down of my own accord' (Jn 10:18). In allowing himself to be crucified, Jesus identified himself with the most oppressed and vilified people of his time. This is the Incarnation brought to its ultimate point of identification with the human condition. If Jesus had not truly suffered, there would have been something lacking in the Incarnation and it would have been harder for us to see him as one like us.

Suffering on its own, however, is something negative. What transforms the horror of the crucifixion into something positive is that it is undertaken out of love and is the means of entry into the new life of resurrection, not only for Jesus, but for the human race. Jesus speaks of his death in terms of being glorified: 'Now my soul is troubled. And what should I say, "Father, save me from this hour"? No, it is for this reason that I have come to this hour. Father, glorify your name' (Jn 12:27-28). He also looks forward to what his death will achieve: 'And I, when I am lifted up from the earth, will draw all people to myself' (Jn 12:32). Johannine spirituality shows no morbid preoccupation with suffering, but accepts suffering as part of the human condition. In the bigger picture of God's plan, it is balanced by something positive. Death leads to resurrection. Sorrow gives way to joy. 'When a woman is in labour, she has pain, because her hour has come. But when her child is born, she no longer remembers the anguish because of the joy of having brought a human being into the world' (Jn 16:21).

Joy is one of the characteristics of Johannine spirituality. It is the joy of knowing that God has shared his life with us. Jesus, the Beloved of the Father, has brought God's love into the world and made it a reality for us. Jesus tells the disciples:

> As the Father has loved me, so I have loved you; abide in my love. If you keep my commandments, you will abide in my love, just as I have kept my Father's commandments and abide in his love. I have said

> these things to you so that my joy may be in you, and that your joy may be complete. (Jn 15:9-11)

The love of the Father and the Son, which has been brought into our midst by the Incarnation, is the life of the Blessed Trinity.

The Blessed Trinity

The Prologue to the Fourth Gospel opens with God 'in the beginning'. Throughout the Gospel, Jesus keeps referring to the Father. So close is the relationship between Jesus and the Father, that Jesus can say to Philip, 'To have seen me is to have seen the Father' (Jn 14:9). Jesus is the image of the Father. Jesus is in the Father and the Father is in him.

Jesus also promises to send the Holy Spirit. 'I will ask the Father, and he will give you another Advocate, to be with you forever'(Jn 14:16). The Holy Spirit is described in personal terms. It is in the Fourth Gospel that the Holy Spirit is most clearly presented as a distinct Person of the Blessed Trinity. He will testify to Jesus. He will lead the disciples into the truth. He will enable them to be witnesses to Jesus. The Advocate is the Spirit of truth. He will lead the disciples to the fullness of truth, by reminding them of the teaching of Jesus.[1]

While the Persons of the Blessed Trinity are clearly delineated as distinct, what is also emphasised is their unity. Jesus and the Father are one. The Son can do nothing of himself. He does only what he is told by the Father.[2] Similarly, the Advocate – the Holy Spirit – does not speak on his own, but what he hears. He takes what belongs to Jesus and declares it. The Holy Spirit glorifies Jesus.[3]

Unity

The unity which is at the heart of the Blessed Trinity is something that Jesus gives to his disciples. He prays that they may be one:

> I ask not only on behalf of these, but also on behalf of those who will believe in me through their word, that they may all be one. As you, Father, are in me and I am in you, may they also be in us, so that the world may believe that you have sent me. (Jn 17:20-21)

So, it is clear that Johannine spirituality is a spirituality of unity. This unity is a unity of love. The sharing of the disciples in the gift of unity is a sharing in the love that Jesus receives from the Father:

> The glory that you have given me I have given them, so that they may be one, as we are one, I in them and you in me, that they may become completely one, so that the world may know that you have sent me and have loved them even as you have loved me. (Jn 17:22-23)

This unity is achieved through love, by putting love into practice.

Unity is not primarily about structures or organisation. It is about love. Putting love into practice in a community will require some organisation and some rules, but these are secondary and at the service of love. John, in fact, does not emphasise the structural or hierarchical element in the

Church. He includes it in the three-fold commission to Peter to tend and feed the Lord's lambs and sheep.[4] But it is clearly subordinate to love. Jesus asks Peter three times 'Do you love me?' before each commissioning. Love is the qualification for any office in the community.

The disciple whom Jesus loved has a privileged place. He shows more insight than Peter. He believes in the resurrection without seeing the Lord.[5] He is the first to recognise the Lord when Jesus appears on the shore of the lake when the disciples have gone fishing in the period after the resurrection.[6] Love gives him a knowledge of the heart. We are told that Jesus loved Martha and her sister and Lazarus.[7] This gives Martha the confidence to ask the Lord to raise her brother to life.[8]

At the Last Supper Jesus gives the disciples a new commandment: 'Love one another. Just as I have loved you, you also should love one another' (Jn 13:34). At the same time, Jesus demonstrates this by washing the disciples' feet. This is an acted out parable. Actions have a more lasting impact on the imagination than words. The ancient prophets, Jeremiah and Ezekiel, also performed dramatic actions to underline their message.[9] Jesus shows that love is very practical. It is expressed in service. It involves taking the initiative, in being the first to love, as Jesus was.

The First Letter of John also spells out the meaning of love:

> Beloved, let us love one another, because love is from God; everyone who loves is born of God and knows God. Whoever does not love does not know God, for God is love. God's love was

> revealed among us in this way: God sent his only Son into the world so that we might live through him. In this is love, not that we loved God but that he loved us and sent his Son to be the atoning sacrifice for our sins. (1 Jn 4:7-12)

It is God who takes the initiative. Our love is a response to what he has done. We show our love for God by loving one another.

Discipleship

Discipleship is an important category in the Fourth Gospel. The Gospel is based on the testimony of the disciple whom Jesus loved.[10] His significance lies in his relationship with Jesus, not in any office he may have held. Traditionally the Beloved Disciple has been identified with the apostle John, son of Zebedee, but the Gospel itself never names him.[11] Being unnamed he becomes the ideal disciple. His faithfulness can be imitated by believers in every age.

The disciples are chosen by Jesus. They become his friends. He reveals to them what he has learnt from the Father.[12] The disciples are to live out the new commandment. 'By this everyone will know that you are my disciples, if you have love for one another' (Jn 13:35). Mutual love is to be their defining characteristic.

The disciples are those who believe in Jesus. In the Fourth Gospel, Martha is the disciple who makes the supreme act of faith, comparable to that of Peter in the Synoptic Gospels. She says: 'Lord, I believe that you are the Messiah, the Son of God, the one coming into the world' (Jn 11:27).

The Place of Mary

Mary features twice in St John's Gospel. On both occasions she is referred to, not by her name, but as 'the mother of Jesus' and on both occasions she is addressed by Jesus with the title 'Woman'. The first occasion is the wedding feast of Cana where Mary draws Jesus' attention to the embarrassing situation that has arisen.[13] She is the one who takes the initiative in a series of actions that will involve Jesus performing his first miracle, and will culminate in his glory being made manifest to his disciples, thus confirming their faith.

The miracle itself is highly symbolic, as the prophets had depicted the future time when God would reign as a wedding feast and a time of plenty. Jesus' action is another way of saying: 'The Kingdom of God has arrived.' The title 'Woman' reminds us of Eve, who also took the initiative, but in that case the end result was the expulsion of human beings from the Garden of Eden. By assenting to become the mother of Jesus, Mary made the redemption of the human race possible. At Cana she sets Jesus on the road to his 'hour,' the hour when this will be achieved.

The second appearance of Mary is beside the Cross.[14] John says that she was 'standing near the cross of Jesus' (Jn 19:25). This simple statement enables us to see this woman of faith and courage standing by her son to the very end. His hour is hers also. She suffers as he does and, indeed, he feels for her as well. Here her role is silent and passive, but like so many mothers in similar situations, her presence is all-important.

The mother of Jesus receives the Beloved Disciple as her son, and so becomes the Mother of the Church. Although the scene is that of a death, it is also paradoxically a birth. The piercing of Christ's side by the soldier is described in terms of a birth: 'at once blood and water came out'(Jn 19:34). The Evangelist draws attention to it as a moment of particular significance by emphasising that it is the account of an eyewitness. This is the mysterious birth of the Church, the fruit of Jesus' death and already present in the community formed by Mary and the Beloved Disciple. 'Unless a grain of wheat falls into the earth and dies, it remains just a single grain; but if it dies, it bears much fruit' (Jn 12:24).

These two incidents frame the activity of Jesus during his public life. It takes place within the context provided by the Woman. She is there at the beginning providing the stimulus that will set the whole drama in motion. She is there again at the end, receiving the fruit of what Jesus has achieved. The spirituality of St John's Gospel has a Marian character. It is totally focused on Jesus, but Mary provides the context within which our relationship with Jesus takes place. Mary is the guarantor of the reality of the Incarnation: Jesus is fully human, because he is born of a woman.

The Sacraments and the Liturgy

The Incarnation is continued in the sacraments. Through the sacraments the glorified Christ is present in his Church. In the conversation with Nicodemus Jesus talks about Baptism.[15] This is not just a ritual of conversion or initiation, but the entry into new life. Jesus speaks of it here in terms of a new birth, being born of water and the Spirit. 'Very truly, I tell you, no one can enter the kingdom of God without being born of water and Spirit' (Jn 3:5). Jesus also uses the image of the wind. Those who are born of the Spirit are animated by a mysterious source of energy.

The image of new birth is a very concrete one. The significance of water as the vehicle through which the Holy Spirit brings about this new birth is developed further as the Gospel progresses. In the conversation with the Samaritan woman Jesus says: 'The water that I will give will become in them a spring of water gushing up to eternal life' (Jn 4:14). The practice of drinking the water blessed at the Easter Vigil would seem to derive from this image of the inner spring. This is a beautiful way of renewing our Baptism, as the water is blessed for this purpose.[16]

In Chapter Six, St John's Gospel gives us the most extended piece of Eucharistic doctrine in the New Testament. It is also surely the most sublime. It begins with the miracle of the loaves and fishes in which Jesus feeds the multitude with food for the body. The next day at Capernaum, when the people come back looking for another miracle, he raises their minds to a higher level and tells them to look for food that will last for eternal life. Jesus speaks of himself as the Bread of Life. He invites those who hunger and thirst to come to him. In contrast to the manna given to the Israelites in the desert, this bread gives eternal life. Jesus is the true bread from heaven. He says: 'The bread that I will give for the life of the world is my flesh' (Jn 6:51). When his Jewish hearers started arguing about this and asking how he could do this, Jesus did not answer the question, but went on to speak of his flesh and blood as food and drink in the most realistic terms. Many later disputes among Christians could have been avoided if the Lord's example had been followed and his words accepted in faith. Not only are the flesh and blood of Jesus real food and drink, but they unite the believer with Jesus in the most intimate way. 'Those who eat my flesh and drink my blood abide in me, and I in them' (Jn 6:56). Through the Eucharist we already have eternal life and the promise of being raised up on the last day.

Saint John's Gospel shows an awareness of the liturgy and, in particular, of the Jewish liturgical year. The feasts of Passover, Tabernacles and Dedication provide the context for important moments in the Gospel. The cleansing of the Temple, which this Gospel places at the beginning of Jesus' public life, takes place in the context of the Passover.[17] The miracle of the loaves, with the discourse on the Bread of Life, also takes place at Passover.[18] Finally the death of Jesus takes place at Passover.[19] The Passover was the central celebration of the Jewish year. It celebrated God's saving act of deliverance when he brought the Israelites out of slavery in Egypt. It expressed their faith that God was always with them and their hope that he would be their saviour in the future. Jesus himself is the ultimate expression of God's saving love in the history of Israel and of all peoples. In him the Passover finds its fullest meaning and fulfilment.

In the account of the resurrection of Jesus the significance of Sunday is brought out. The account begins by telling us the time and the day of the week: 'Early on the first day of the week, while it was still dark' (Jn 20:1). When Jesus shows himself to the disciples that evening, we are reminded again, that it is the first day of the week.[20] The second appearance to the assembled disciples, this time including Thomas, is on the following Sunday, the eighth day.[21] When the Gospel came to be written Eucharist and Sunday were already of great significance for Christians.

The 'Johannine Pentecost'

In the Gospel of John the resurrection of Jesus, his ascension and the giving of the Holy Spirit to the disciples all happen on Easter Sunday. As in the other gospels no one sees the resurrection itself, but the risen Jesus shows himself to the disciples. Mary Magdalene and the other women discover the empty tomb and run to tell the disciples. Peter and the other disciple, 'the one Jesus loved', run to the tomb. Peter enters first, but it is the Beloved Disciple who understands the meaning of the discarded grave clothes. Without seeing, he believes that Jesus is risen, because love has its own way of knowing. Mary Magdalene has returned to the tomb and remains there after the others have left. It is then that she encounters Jesus himself. At first she mistakes him for the gardener, but when he calls her by name, she recognises him. She tries to cling onto him, showing that his body is real. His resurrection is real. Jesus tells her to go to his brothers and tell them: 'I am ascending to my Father and your Father, to my God and your God' (Jn 20:17).

On the evening of the same day Jesus appears to the disciples gathered in the upper room. He greets them with the familiar Jewish greeting 'Shalom'. He shows them his hands and his side, demonstrating that he really is risen. Then Jesus does three things which we may see as the 'Johannine Pentecost'. He sends them: 'As the Father has sent me so am I sending you' (Jn 20:21). He breathes on them. He communicates the Holy Spirit to them, saying: 'Receive the Holy Spirit'(Jn 20:22). The disciples are sent forth in the power of the Spirit, the Breath of God, to be instruments of reconciliation, to bring to others the forgiveness of sins which Jesus achieved through his death and resurrection.

In the St Luke's Gospel these same events are presented as having occurred over a period of several weeks. The ascension takes place after forty days and the Holy Spirit comes on the Jewish feast of Pentecost, fifty days after Passover. How are we to understand these two different accounts? Both express the truth, but from different perspectives. John's perspective is theological, whereas Luke's is historical. From a theological perspective the resurrection and ascension are aspects of the one reality and the outpouring of the Holy Spirit is their consequence.

In the case of the ascension John is showing us that from the moment of the resurrection, Jesus is in fact in glory with the Father. Our human nature has been brought to share intimately in the life of the Blessed Trinity, and so the brothers and sisters of Jesus share in his relationship with the Father. His God is our God; his Father is our Father. Luke, on the other hand, focuses on the fact that there was a last occasion when Jesus appeared to the disciples and was taken up into heaven.

In the case of the giving of the Holy Spirit, John is more interested in the interior peace and joy, which the Spirit brings, than in the more dramatic charismatic manifestations such as speaking in tongues. The Holy Spirit is most clearly seen in mutual love:

> This is his commandment, that we should believe in the name of his Son Jesus Christ and love one

> another, just as he has commanded us. All who obey his commandments abide in him, and he abides in them. And by this we know that he abides in us, by the Spirit that he has given us. (1 Jn 3:23-24)

In the Acts of the Apostles the Holy Spirit makes his presence known a number of times, but the most dramatic is at Pentecost when he descends in the form of tongues of fire and sends the apostles out to proclaim the good news about Jesus. The Church, which was born from the side of Christ as he died on the Cross, is made manifest to the world at Pentecost. This is the beginning of the mission of the Church.

Perhaps the relationship between what I have called the 'Johannine Pentecost' and the event of Pentecost itself, as recounted by Luke in the Acts of the Apostles, may be explained by a common experience. We receive the Holy Spirit in the Sacrament of Confirmation, but very often the experience of the Holy Spirit, or of the working of his gifts, comes much later. The disciples received the Holy Spirit on Easter Sunday, but it was at Pentecost that they experienced his power and the charismatic gifts which enabled them to preach, to bear witness and to work miracles.

Not only do the events of Easter Sunday form a unity in themselves, but they are also inseparable from the death of Jesus on the Cross, which he refers to as his 'hour'. The resurrection appearance to the disciples, including Thomas, clearly shows this. Thomas was not present on the first occasion when Jesus showed himself to the gathering of disciples. He said he would not believe that Jesus was risen unless he could see and touch the holes in his hands and the wound in his side. When Jesus appears eight days later, he invites Thomas to probe the wounds that his body still bears even in its glorified state. By drawing attention to the wounds of the crucifixion, Thomas has reminded us that the Risen One is at the same time the One who was Crucified. The resurrection did not come about except through the great labour and suffering of the Cross.

Prayer

Saint John's Gospel shows us Jesus praying to the Father. Before raising Lazarus from the dead, Jesus raises his eyes to heaven and says: 'Father, I thank you for having heard me. I knew that you always hear me, but I have said this for the sake of the crowd standing here, so that they may believe that you sent me' (Jn 11:41-42). Prayer is just a glance towards heaven. There is no need for many words, because the Father already knows what Jesus wants and has already granted it. This is strikingly in keeping with Jesus' teaching on prayer in St Matthew's Gospel.[22]

The great example of prayer in St John's Gospel is the priestly prayer of Jesus in Chapter 17. Again Jesus begins by raising his eyes to heaven and addresses God as Father. Jesus prays that the Father be glorified. He prays for the disciples, that they be protected, that they be sanctified and that they be made one.

In the discourse at the Last Supper, Jesus tells the disciples to pray to the Father in his name. 'Very truly, I tell you, if you ask anything of the Father in my name, he will give it to you'(Jn 16:23). Such is the unity between the disciples and Jesus, and between Jesus and the Father that the disciples can pray directly to the Father. 'On that day you will ask in my name. I do not say to you that I will ask the Father on your behalf; for the Father himself loves you, because you have loved me and have believed that I came from God'(Jn 16:26-27).

We can also pray directly to Jesus. This is in keeping with the entire thrust of the Gospel which presents Jesus as God incarnate, the image of the Father. At the beginning of his public life, Jesus invites the disciples to 'come and see' (Jn 1:39). During the celebration of the Feast of Tabernacles, he calls to the crowd: 'Let anyone who is thirsty come to me' (Jn 7:37). At the Last Supper, he says: 'I am the way, the truth and the life' (Jn 14:6).

The Holy Spirit also has a role in our prayer. When Jesus returns to the Father, it is the Holy Spirit who supports and accompanies the disciples. Jesus, as an historical person, was with them for a time, but the Spirit will remain always.[23] At the Last Supper he tells the disciples: 'It is to your advantage that I go away, for if I do not go away, the Advocate will not come to you; but if I go, I will send him to you' (Jn 16:7).

Jesus goes on to explain to the disciples that after his glorification, he will be present in a new way, through the Holy Spirit.

> You know him, because he abides with you, and he will be in you. I will not leave you orphaned; I am coming to you. In a little while the world will no longer see me, but you will see me; because I live, you also will live. On that day you will know that I am in my Father, and you in me and I in you. (Jn 14:17-20)

In the abiding presence of the Holy Spirit, we are united with Jesus, and in him also with the Father. It follows that we may also pray to the Holy Spirit. All prayer is a privileged sharing in the life of the Blessed Trinity.

The teaching on prayer, whether directed to Jesus or to the Father, is often interpreted in individualistic terms. This interpretation is not incorrect, in that it is certainly important that the individual believer pray to God and have a personal relationship with Jesus. However, this teaching is directed to the disciples as a group. It is given in the context of the new commandment to love and of Jesus' promise to send the Holy Spirit. This teaching of Jesus on prayer immediately precedes his own prayer that the disciples may all be one. So it may be more appropriate to see this teaching as primarily referring to communal prayer and liturgical prayer. Over the past few centuries there has been too much emphasis on the individualistic aspects of spirituality and not enough on the communal.

A Spirituality of Communion

It is a characteristic of our times that human beings have become more and more isolated and, yet, the yearning for meaningful relationships has never been greater. This can be observed in popular culture. It is the theme of films, songs and literature. Human beings search for love, but it eludes them. The answer to this thirst for love and meaning is to be found in communion.

The Greek word *koinõnia* means sharing something in common. It is translated as 'fellowship' or 'communion'. The Gospel message is given to us so that we may share in the life of God, the life that Jesus brought to us by sharing our life. We then share this life with one another. 'We declare to you what we have seen and heard so that you also may have fellowship with us; and truly our fellowship is with the Father and with his Son Jesus Christ' (1 Jn 1:3). The communion, which is the life of the Blessed Trinity, is brought into the world through the Incarnation and we share in it through our life of faith. This life of faith is celebrated in the sacraments and the liturgy. It is lived out in mutual love. It is supported by the communion of saints in which Mary has the first place. John's message is one of joy for an angst-ridden world. 'We are writing these things so that our joy may be complete' (1 Jn 1:4).

The Johannine Influence on Irish Spirituality

The spirituality and theology of St John came to the West through the dissemination of the Gospel and Letters of John. The Book of Revelation, although probably written by a different John, also came from the same milieu. The Johannine tradition also spread through personal contact. There were trading links between the Rhône valley in Gaul and Asia Minor. There were Greek-speaking communities in Marseille, Nice and Lyons. In the second century St Irenaeus came from Smyrna and became Bishop of Lyons. Growing up in Smyrna, he had been taught by its bishop, St Polycarp, who in turn had been taught by St John. This gave the Church in Gaul a direct link with the Apostolic Tradition.

There were close links between Christians in Ireland and those in Gaul from the start. The original Christian community in Ireland, to which Pope Celestine sent Palladius as first bishop,[24] may have originated in a group of Christian refugees from Gaul fleeing persecution in the Roman Empire. In any case, early missionaries to Ireland, including St Patrick, either came from Gaul or spent some time there. The Irish Christians regarded themselves as disciples of St Peter and St Paul. They also felt they had a connection with St John.[25]

I have already mentioned that the practice of drinking the water when visiting a holy well shows the influence of St John's Gospel, as does the similar practice of drinking the water blessed at the Easter Vigil. This influence can be seen in other ways as well.

It can be seen in the Irish high crosses.[26] In St John's Gospel, Jesus refers to his crucifixion as his being lifted up, his glorification. On the high crosses he is depicted in this way, often in the seamless robe of the high priest. Mary and John are usually included as well, and sometimes a larger group representing the Church. There are very few separate images of the resurrection, because the death on the cross is presented in such a way as to include the resurrection. This shows a profound understanding of the Paschal Mystery.[27]

Only in St John's Gospel are we told that, after his death on the Cross, Christ's side was pierced with a lance. In medieval Irish piety there was a devotion to the wounds of Christ and in particular to the wound in his side. In the eighteenth century this tendency to meditate on the wounded Christ was developed further in the devotion to the Sacred Heart of Jesus. This came about mainly through the influence of St Margaret Mary Alacoque who experienced visions of the Sacred Heart of Jesus at Paray-le-Monial in France in 1675. The devotion was brought to

Ireland by members of the Jesuit Order and other priests educated in France.[28] The devotion fitted in perfectly with the Irish approach to the humanity of Christ. It is also thoroughly Johannine. A fine example of this piety is to be found in the poem *Gile mo chroí* by Tadhg Gaelach Ó Súileabháin:

> Gile mo chroí do chroí-se, a Shlánaitheoir,
> Is ciste mo chroí do chroí-se d'fháil im' chomhair.
> Ós follas gur líon do chroí dem' ghrá-sa, a stór,
> I gcochall mo chroí do chroí-se fág i gcomhad.
>
> The light of my heart is your heart, O Saviour mine,
> And my heart's greatest treasure is your heart poured out for me.
> And seeing that your heart is so full of love, a Stóir,
> In the folds of my poor heart leave yours entwined with mine.[29]
> (Translated by Dónal O'Connor)

This poem also exemplifies another Johannine theme, that of light. This crops up frequently in Irish prayers and poems. Christ is often addressed as 'A Rí ghil' ('O bright King').

Another feature of Irish spirituality that shows its Johannine character is the strong devotion to Mary. Mary was entrusted to the beloved disciple at the foot of the Cross. In this connection it was fitting that St John himself appeared at Knock along with Our Lady and St Joseph.

I have always found it interesting that the visionaries identified the figure of the bishop with the book as St John. The vision of the Lamb on the altar surrounded by angels resonates with the words of St John the Baptist, with which Jesus is introduced at the start of the Gospel: 'Behold the Lamb of God' (Jn 1:29). It also reminds us of the Lamb in the Book of Revelation.[30]

The Mass has always been central to Irish spirituality. For many centuries the words of Thomas 'My Lord and my God' were used by Irish people at the elevation of the Host as a spontaneous expression of faith in the crucified and risen Lord really present in the Blessed Sacrament. When the Mass in the vernacular was introduced, these words were included as a memorial acclamation for use in Ireland.[31] It was a recognition of the continuing influence of St John's Gospel.

NOTES

1. John 14:16, 27.
2. John 8:28.
3. John 16:13-15.
4. John 21:15-17.
5. John 20:8.
6. John 21:7.
7. John 11:15.
8. John 11:21-22.
9. E.g. Jeremiah 27:1-22 and Ezekiel 12:1-20.
10. John 21:24.
11. Saint Irenaeus identifies the Beloved Disciple as the apostle John. Cf. Michael Mullins, *The Gospel of John A Commentary*, pp. 23–5. Other possible identities for the Beloved Disciple have been suggested, such as another disciple also called John, or Lazarus, to whom his sisters refer as 'the one you love' (Jn 11:3).
12. John 15:14-16.

13. John 2:1-12.
14. John 19:25-27.
15. John 3:1-8.
16. Cf. Eoin de Bhaldraithe, *The High Crosses of Moone and Castledermot* (Athy: Rainsford Publishing, 2009), p. 38.
17. John 2:13.
18. John 6:4.
19. John 19:42.
20. John 20:19.
21. John 20:26.
22. Cf. Mt 6:7-9.
23. Cf. Jn 14:15.
24. Cf. The Chronicle of Prosper of Aquitaine in Liam de Paor, *St Patrick's World* (Dublin: Four Courts Press), p. 79.
25. For instance, at the Synod of Whitby in 664 AD while defending the Irish system for calculating the date of Easter, Colman claimed that the Irish were following a tradition handed down from St John. Cf. St Bede, Ecclesiastical History, bk. 3, ch. 25.
26. Cf. Oliver Crilly, *The Great Irish Crosses: Meaning and Mystery* (Dublin: Columba Press, 2013).
27. The Paschal Mystery and its implications for spirituality are discussed more fully in Chapter Six.
28. Cf. Úna Nic Einrí, *An Cantaire Siúlach: Tadhg Gaelach* (An Daingean: An Sagart, 2001), pp. 52–6.
29. Dónal O'Connor DD, *Ardmore & Lismore Early Irish Spirituality in the Decies*, third edition (Ardmore, 2001), p. 13.
30. Cf. Rev 5:6-14. Cf. Eoin de Bhaldraithe, *The Apparition at Knock, The Ecumenical Dimension* (Moone: Bolton Abbey, 2013), pp. 22–38.
31. *An Leabhar Aifreann* was published in 1973 and the *Roman Missal* in 1975.

CHAPTER SIX

FINDING GOD IN ALL THINGS

The title of this chapter is taken from a phrase often used by St Ignatius of Loyola which expresses well his belief that it is possible to find God in all aspects of our lives. This is really the purpose of spirituality. In this chapter I want to look at the practical question of how we might cultivate spirituality so that we would, in fact, find God in our own lives. Christian spirituality is the lived experience of faith in God, Father, Son and Holy Spirit. So what we are asking is: how can we deepen our relationship with God and allow it to have an impact on all aspects of life?

Saint Teresa of Ávila says that there are three things necessary for those who seek the way of prayer. This applies to spirituality in general as well. 'The first of these is love for one another; the second is detachment from all created things; the third is true humility.'[1] Christian spirituality takes as its starting point the commandment to love given by Jesus. Detachment means having a proper respect for other persons and for created things, based on a true appreciation of their value. It means to care without being possessive. It is not to be confused with indifference. Humility is about having a true appraisal of ourselves. It is not about having low self-esteem. The Magnificat is the most perfect expression of humility. In this hymn of praise Mary acknowledges the great things God has done for her, but does not attribute her greatness to herself but gives thanks to God for it.

All knowledge of God and all growth in our relationship with him depend on grace. We cannot make it happen: it is God's gift. However, the very fact that we are interested in having a deeper relationship with God means that grace is already at work in us. We can cooperate with God's grace and we can be helped in doing so by drawing on the wisdom of those who have trodden this path before us. One of the things I have been stressing in the previous chapters of this book is that we belong to a tradition. That tradition has left us ways in which spirituality has been cultivated by the pilgrims, prophets and wise people who went before us. Let us now look at some of these.

The Liturgy

In the liturgy the eternal breaks into time. The sacrifice of Christ offered historically on Calvary is made present for us in the Mass, so that we can be taken up into it. For God all reality, past, present and future, is one. The life, death, resurrection, ascension and glorious return of Christ are realities which are present to God. In the Mass we say 'we remember' and 'we look forward', but what is actually happening is much greater than a simple remembering or looking forward. We are brought in touch with these realities in a real, but mysterious way. Time is transcended.

Taking part in the Mass must have pride of place in any attempt to open ourselves to the mystery of Christ. Through the Mass we are progressively drawn into the mystery of Christ. Many people have discovered this without necessarily articulating it very clearly. This explains why so many people have remained faithful to the Mass down through the centuries. Holy Communion is a deeply mystical experience for many.

The Blessed Sacrament reserved in our churches is also a precious gift. Most churches are open all day, so that people can pray to the Lord present in the Eucharist. Many people also spend extended periods in adoration.

The liturgy also includes the Prayer of the Church or Liturgy of the Hours. What is distinctive about this prayer is that it is related to particular times of the day and so is a means of sanctifying time itself. It is a manifestation of the Church at prayer. The Church is the body of Christ: Christ the Head and the members of his body united to him. The Prayer of the Church consists mainly of the Psalms and some other biblical canticles. The Psalms are the prayer of Christ.

Taking part in the liturgy on a regular basis brings us into the great movement of the Church's year. The heart of the liturgical year is the Easter Vigil, when we celebrate the passage of Christ from the ultimate point of self-emptying, which is his death on the Cross, to his glorification in his resurrection from the dead. This is called the Paschal Mystery. The term 'mystery' is used here in the sense in which we speak of the 'Mysteries of the Rosary'. A mystery is an event that can only be appreciated from the perspective of faith. Our understanding of it never completely exhausts its meaning. This passage from suffering, through death to new life, is Christ's Passover. The word 'Paschal' comes from *pascha*, the Greek word for Passover. Christ's Passover becomes our passover through Baptism. This is why the Easter Vigil is the most appropriate occasion on which to be baptised.

The rest of the liturgical year is the unpacking of what is celebrated in the Easter Vigil. The liturgical year is like a pond into which a stone has been dropped that sends out ripples. The most immediate ripple is the Easter Triduum: an unpacking over three days dedicated to Christ crucified (Friday), buried (Saturday) and risen (Sunday) with the celebration of the Lord's Supper (Thursday evening) as a prelude or overture.[2] The next ripple gives us Holy Week leading up to the *Triduum* and the Easter Octave which is the extension of Easter Sunday to the following Sunday. During the Octave one of the accounts of the resurrection is read each day. The Easter Season is a further unpacking bringing us to Pentecost, which celebrates the gift of the Holy Spirit, the fruit of the Paschal Mystery. Lent is a preparation for Easter and, especially during Holy Week, gives us the opportunity to meditate on the sufferings of Christ, the aspect of the Paschal Mystery which is his self-emptying.

The Paschal Mystery is celebrated throughout the year, as every Sunday is a 'little Easter' and every Friday is a day of penance. At first sight the celebration of Christ's birth at Christmas, along with Advent and Christmastide, would seem to be an exception to this. However, the Incarnation is the beginning of the Paschal Mystery. God the Son had to become a human being first, before he could die and rise again.

The significance of the Paschal Mystery for spirituality is that, just as it was the pattern of Christ's life, it is also the pattern of our lives. We experience suffering, failure and disappointment, but we also experience being lifted up. The Cross is part of our lives, but we also experience resurrection.

Reading Scripture

Reading Scripture is another activity that cultivates spirituality. The purpose of this reading is to listen to the Word of God. The reading itself is of value because it brings one into contact with God's Word. The aim is not to cover a lot of material, but to let God's Word sink into our hearts so that we are led into prayer. 'Whoever loves me will keep my word' (Jn 14:24).

The method called *Lectio divina* can help us here. The late Cardinal Martini gives a good explanation of this method in his book *The Joy of the Gospel: Meditations for Young People.* Basically there are three steps in this approach. These are *lectio*, *meditatio* and *contemplatio.*

Lectio means reading. It involves selecting a passage and reading it carefully. Then I ask the question, 'What is this passage of Scripture about?' What did it mean in its original setting? What is it saying?

Meditatio means meditation. This step involves entering into dialogue with God's Word. I ask the question: 'What is this passage saying to me?'

This leads to the third step which Martini describes as follows: '*Contemplatio* is adoration, praise, silence in the presence of him who is the ultimate object of my prayer, Christ the Lord.'[3]

Prayer and Contemplation

Further useful advice on this third step can be got from St Teresa of Ávila. Her book *The Way of Perfection* is particularly useful as she wrote it to help beginners in prayer. Saint Teresa had the knack of getting to the heart of the matter. In her project of returning to a simpler form of religious life, the principal concept that she employed was that of friendship. 'All should be friends, all should be cherished, all should be cared for.' She applied the same concept to prayer. 'Mental prayer is nothing else than an intimate sharing between friends.' Prayer is a relationship.

Saint Teresa offered this advice to those who find it hard to concentrate and who are plagued by distractions. She says, as you are alone, choose a companion. What better companion than the Lord?

> Represent the Lord Himself as close to you and behold how lovingly and humbly he is teaching you. Believe me: you should remain with so good a friend as long as you can.[4]

She goes on to say that we do not have to weary ourselves either with much thinking or much talking, but simply to focus our attention on the Lord.

> I am not asking you to do any more than look at Him. For who can keep you from turning the eyes of your soul toward this Lord, even if you do so just for a moment if you can't do more?[5]

A distinction is often made between 'vocal prayer' and 'mental prayer'. By the former is meant the use of set prayers which we have learnt or which we find in prayer books. Mental prayer is when we pray freely from our own thoughts and feelings. The recitation of vocal prayers has often been compared unfavourable with mental prayer.

This is because they are often 'rattled off' without engaging the mind and heart. When they are said properly, however, vocal prayers can be of great value. As in our conversations with each other, the important thing in our conversation with the Lord is attentiveness. Saint Teresa says that when vocal prayer is said with recollection it has, in fact, become mental prayer. She goes on to say:

> To keep you from thinking that little is gained through the perfect recitation of vocal prayer, I tell you that it is very possible that while you are reciting the Our Father or some other vocal prayer, the Lord may raise you to perfect contemplation.[6]

The Our Father is the most important vocal prayer, because it was given to us by the Lord himself. It admits us to his own experience of God as 'Abba'. The Psalms are also the prayer of Jesus. Not only are they prayers that he would have used during his earthly life, but they are now the main component in the Prayer of the Church, the prayer which the Body of Christ offers in his name. Prayers composed by the saints are also useful, because these are the prayers of people who knew God.

The Rosary combines vocal prayer, meditation and contemplation. The vocal prayers are the Our Father, Hail Mary and Glory be to the Father said on the beads. Meditation is provided by the Mysteries which one pictures in the mind or reflects upon. These include all the main events in the life of Our Lord. Underlying all this, the Rosary is a way of spending time in the presence of God, which is contemplation. The Rosary is also a way of praying with

Mary, who as Mother of Christ and Mother of the Church plays an indispensable part in our lives.

Spirituality is not just about prayer, but about the whole of life. At the same time if we want to develop our relationship with God, prayer will be an important part of that development. The real test of whether we are making progress in prayer is the quality of our relationships. The life of prayer is sometimes seen as a flight from reality, but it is, in fact, the very opposite. It is living contact with reality. For instance, one of the basic tenets of our faith is that God is everywhere. Prayer should enable us to live according to this truth and find God in all things. So, if one has the right attitude, it makes no difference whether one is sweeping the floor or helping a neighbour or saying one's prayers: God is glorified in whatever one is doing. It is through prayer that we are gradually enabled to see life whole in this way.

Attentiveness

One of the difficulties that many people experience is being distracted at prayer. This is part of a larger problem, namely, that we are distracted in our lives generally. We do not give our full attention to what we are doing or saying. For instance, if I am having a conversation with someone, instead of listening carefully to what the other person is saying, often I am thinking of what I am going to say next myself or my mind is on something completely different. The culture we live in does not help. It fills our consciousness with images and sounds. We need to rediscover the beauty of silence. Maybe we can create moments of silence, little oases of peace in the midst of all the noise and activity. Most people are afraid of silence, because it seems like emptiness, but it is only against a background of silence that we can really listen.

We need to slow down and pay attention to the present moment. If we are living in the present moment, we are in touch with reality. Only the present is real. It is also where God is to be found. God is the ground holding all reality together. The present moment is also the gateway to eternity. Time is a condition of our limited existence. 'Now' is the only part of time that we can actually be in, but it is also the part of time that opens onto eternity, because God holds both dimensions together. T. S. Eliot calls it 'the point of intersection of the timeless with time'.[7]

Fasting

In September 2013, when the civil war in Syria looked like it was escalating into an international conflict, possibly even a third world war, Pope Francis called for a day of prayer and fasting. This call was responded to with prayer vigils and fasting held all over the world. In the following week the situation changed dramatically. The United States and Russia agreed to work together to end the conflict and the Syrian government agreed to get rid of chemical weapons. Even though the war in Syria continued, a wider conflict was avoided and there was now real hope that peace could be achieved. It was a remarkable demonstration of the power of prayer.

An interesting aspect of this initiative by Pope Francis was the linking of prayer with fasting. There are many examples of this in the Bible. When the Jewish people in Persia were threatened with extermination by the plots of an evil court official, Esther took her life in her hands in order to petition the king to spare the Jews. It was not permitted, under pain of death, to enter the presence of the king unbidden. Before she went to the king, Esther told her uncle Mordecai to assemble all the Jews and to ask them to fast for three days. They fasted and prayed for deliverance.[8]

Joel also called for fasting and prayer in the face of national calamity. He envisaged a liturgical assembly:

> Blow the trumpet in Zion; sanctify a fast, call a solemn assembly; gather the people. Sanctify the congregation; assemble the aged; gather the children, even infants at the breast. (Jl 2:15-17)

It is appropriate that this passage is read on Ash Wednesday which also has the combination of fasting, assembly and prayer.

In the Book of Tobit, which beautifully evokes the spirituality of the Jews of the Dispersion, Raphael says to Tobit: 'Prayer with fasting is good, but better than both is almsgiving with righteousness' (Tob 12:8). Again prayer is linked with fasting and here a third practice is added, that of almsgiving.

There are also examples in the New Testament. Anna, the daughter of Phanuel, who was present when the Lord was brought to the temple, served God day and night with fasting and prayer.[9] Barnabas and Saul were chosen for their missionary work in the context of liturgical prayer and fasting.

> While they were worshipping the Lord and fasting, the Holy Spirit said: 'Set apart for me

> Barnabas and Saul for the work to which I have called them.' Then after fasting and praying they laid their hands on them and sent them off. (Acts 13:2-3)

It is apparent from these examples that fasting lends a particular intensity to prayer. In fact fasting itself becomes a prayer, a way in which the body joins in the prayer of the mind.

Jesus himself fasted and prayed. The period of forty days he spent in the desert in preparation for his ministry was a recapitulation of the forty years that the people of Israel spent in the desert before entering the Promised Land.[10] Jesus took it for granted that his followers would fast, but he did not place any particular emphasis on it and he warned against making a show of it.[11]

The early Christians fasted on Wednesdays and Fridays.[12] In Irish the names for these days of the week come from this. *Céadaoin* (Wednesday) means 'First Fast', *Aoine* (Friday) means 'Fast', while the *Déardaoin* (Thursday) means 'day between two fasts'. For most of the Church's history Lent was the main period of fasting. Fasting meant taking only one meal and also the exclusion of certain foods, such as meat, eggs and dairy products.[13] Fridays throughout the year were days of abstinence. Abstinence involved not eating meat or meat products. Since 1917 fasting has involved the reduction of food intake to one meal and two collations (what we might call 'snacks').

Unfortunately, when fasting came to be seen as an end in itself and as an obligation that had been imposed, many people became very scrupulous about it. Canonists discussed how much one might take in a 'collation' or whether one could have a biscuit with a cup of tea. Bishops issued rulings on these questions at the beginning of Lent.[14] Inevitably, this led to the whole practice of fasting being brought into disrepute and so obligatory fasting was reduced to just two days (Ash Wednesday and Good Friday) after the Second Vatican Council. In effect, fasting was dropped for a generation. This was necessary in order to get away from the legalistic morass in which it had become bogged down. However, fasting is part of our tradition and is a valuable spiritual discipline. The time is now ripe for it to be rediscovered.

Fasting is not about despising the body or punishing it. Fasting is a way of taking the body seriously and making it part of the spiritual life. The body itself must be sanctified and prepared for resurrection. It seems to me that the proper context for fasting is in solidarity with other Christians and combined with prayer. This was its original context. There were certain days when people fasted and these were days of more intense prayer. Taking on fasting on an individual basis can be dangerous as it can lead to eating disorders. It should only be done in consultation with one's spiritual director. It is also wise to follow the guidelines laid down by the Church, such as taking one proper meal on fast days.

Over the centuries fasting came to be associated more with penance than with prayer. It was seen as a way of expressing sorrow for one's sins. The exception to this was the Eucharistic fast. This was a way of expressing a hunger for God. The traditional fast was from the night before receiving Holy Communion at morning Mass. The introduction of evening Mass necessitated a modification of the traditional fast. Since the 1960s it has been reduced to one hour. This is not so much a fast as a way of showing respect for the Eucharist by separating it from the taking of ordinary food.

Be Converted Every Day

If we are to grow spiritually, we need to grow in self-knowledge. There are two means which will help us in this quest. These are the Sacrament of Reconciliation and the practice of spiritual direction. The Sacrament of Reconciliation is a meeting with the Lord in which we confess our sins and receive forgiveness. Through it we are given grace to overcome our faults. The sacrament itself needs to be part of an ongoing conversion where every day we try to follow the Lord more closely.

Spiritual direction means sharing our spiritual journey with someone with whom we can be honest and who can help us to see what God is doing in our lives. In early Irish monasticism the spiritual director was called *anamchara*, meaning 'soulfriend.' Many people also find it very helpful to keep a journal.

Sharing One's Faith

Christian faith is deeply personal, but it is not private. By its nature it is communal. It is lived out in the community which is the Church. Getting more involved in the life of one's parish helps to build up one's faith. Often this takes the form of joining a group of some kind. There are prayer groups, apostolic groups, branches of movements and groups associated with religious orders. All of them help to focus one's spirituality in a particular way. Often divine providence arranges for one to come in contact with such a group. For instance, a friend might invite you to come with them to a meeting.

All of these groups give one the opportunity to share one's faith. We are pilgrims on the journey of life. We need the support of each other. We are also missionaries. Pope Francis emphasises this point in his Apostolic Exhortation, *Evangelii Gaudium* (The Joy of the Gospel).

> In virtue of their Baptism, all members of the People of God have become missionary disciples (cf. Mt 28:19). All the baptised, whatever their position in the Church or their level of instruction in the faith, are agents of evangelisation, and it would be insufficient to envisage a plan of evangelisation to be carried out by professionals while the rest of the faithful would simply be passive recipients. The new evangelisation calls for personal involvement on the part of each of the baptised.
>
> The Samaritan woman became a missionary immediately after speaking with Jesus and many Samaritans came to believe in him 'because of the woman's testimony' (Jn 4:39). So too, St Paul, after his encounter with Jesus Christ, 'immediately proclaimed Jesus' (Acts 9:20; cf. 22: 6-21). So what are we waiting for?[15]

A Contemporary Irish Spirituality

Has the Irish tradition a distinctive contribution to make to spirituality? We should not be looking for something distinctively Irish in order to be different, but we should see it as a source of richness to be shared. There is a rich heritage of Irish Christianity going back to the fifth century and possibly earlier. The Christian faith has become part of the Irish psyche. A visitor to Ireland would notice the impact of Christianity even on the landscape, where it is evident in the ancient high crosses and round towers and in more recently built churches. It is also evident in people's outlook and in their speech. This is particularly so in the Irish language where even everyday greetings contain references to God, but it is also to be found in English where expressions like, 'It is a fine day, thank God', are so common that we do not notice them.

One word that might be used to characterise Irish spirituality is 'incarnational'. We looked at the idea of the Incarnation in the context of St John's Gospel. It means that God became a human being like us and so he is very near. God is our friend. We can talk to him in an intimate way. We find this in the traditional Irish prayers and it is still a living reality for many people. The Incarnation also implies that God is present in our neighbour. 'Neighbourliness', *muintearas* in Irish, may not be a word used in theology, but it expresses in a down-to-earth way what theological terms like *communio* or *koinõnia* are about. This neighbourliness is not inward looking or 'clannish', but includes the idea of welcoming the stranger. A visitor to Ireland would notice the strong sense of community. It is particularly evident at funerals. Funerals are occasions of neighbourly solidarity.

There was a kind of ecumenism of neighbourliness, before that term became familiar. People of different traditions respected and helped one another, particularly in the country. Unfortunately, where political loyalties became entwined with religious differences, there have also been tensions and misunderstandings. The Ecumenical Movement has helped overcome these misunderstandings and enabled Christians of different traditions to appreciate how much they have in common. In the area of spirituality all Irish Christians share the same basic outlook. There is a sort of down-to-earth authenticity that is common to all Christians in Ireland. All value faith in Christ, regard prayer as very important, practice neighbourliness and believe in a practical Christianity which helps those in need and is oriented to mission. The ultimate goal of Ecumenism is the reunification of the Churches. While this may seem to be a long way off, there are intermediate goals that can be achieved. We can be united in mutual love, in our service to those in need, in our witness to Christian values, and we can be united in prayer. The Ecumenism of neighbourliness is still something precious and powerful.

An awareness of the Incarnation naturally leads to an appreciation of sacrament and liturgy. The Eucharist has always been central to Irish spirituality. There are two areas in particular in which a uniquely Irish contribution can be made to the liturgy. These are the celebration of the Irish saints and sacred music.

There are now proper texts for the feast days of the Irish saints. The ideas in these texts are drawn from the lives of the saints. For instance, for the feast of St Columba on 9 June, the collect alludes to the pilgrim people and the preface says that Columba made songs to the glory of God, guided others by the gift of wisdom and became a pilgrim for Christ so that those across the sea might hear the gospel of peace. The traditional blessing attributed to St Columba is also included. These texts are a rich source of Irish spirituality.

Sacred music is an area where Irish culture can make an important contribution to the liturgy. Very good work has been done in developing a native tradition of sacred music since Vatican II. A number of Irish composers have produced settings of the parts of the Mass, of the Psalms and of hymns which are of very good quality. This does not mean abandoning the riches of the Gregorian heritage. As the music proper to the Roman Rite it can continue to be used and also have an influence on the kind of music used in the vernacular. Many of the new compositions show the influence of both Gregorian chant and *sean nós*. It has been amply demonstrated that it is possible to sing the Mass in Irish and in English in a way that is prayerful, evocative and authentically Irish. There is a long and honoured tradition of multilingualism in the liturgy. The traditional Latin liturgy included the use of Greek and Hebrew (*Kyrie eleison* and *Alleluia*). It is possible, for instance, to have Mass in English with sung parts in Latin and hymns in Irish.

There is also the wider sense of the sacramentality of the ordinary which Patrick Kavanagh captured so well in his poetry. God is present in nature and in the happenings of every day. This can suddenly strike us. The word is also a kind of sacrament. The Incarnation begins with the Word (Jn 1:1). Ireland is renowned as a country of poets and writers. We have also produced a good many biblical scholars. Reflecting on the Word of God comes naturally to us. All spirituality must draw on this source. In modern times the Bible has become much more accessible.

In conclusion, I would say that a contemporary Irish spirituality would have a sense of the heritage of the past, with its traditions of prayer, pilgrimage and mission. It would be nourished by the Bible and the liturgy. It would continue to express itself in neighbourliness and in fostering unity. It would be open to the challenges and possibilities of the future. Like the scribe who becomes a disciple of the kingdom of heaven, we will bring out of our treasure 'what is new and what is old' (Mt 13:52).

NOTES

1. Saint Teresa of Ávila, *The Way of Perfection*, ch. 4, 5. Cf. *The Collected Works of St Teresa of Avila*, volume 2, Kieran Kavanaugh OCD and Otilio Rodriguez OCD, trans. (Washington: ICS Publications, 1980).
2. Thursday evening is already Friday from a liturgical point of view, both Jewish and Christian.
3. Cardinal Carlo Maria Martini, *The Joy of the Gospel: Meditations for Young People* (Collegeville: The Liturgical Press, 1994), pp. 2–3.
4. Saint Teresa of Ávila, *The Way of Perfection*, ch. 26, 3.
5. Ibid.
6. St Teresa of Ávila, *The Way of Perfection*, ch. 25, 1.
7. T. S. Eliot, 'The Dry Salvages', *Collected Poems 1909–1962* (Faber & Faber, 1963), p. 213.
8. Esther 4:15-17.
9. Luke 2:37.
10. Matthew 4:1-2; Luke 4:1-2.
11. Matthew 6:16-18.
12. *Didache* 8.

13. Pancakes were made on Shrove Tuesday to use up eggs which would not be eaten during Lent. Having an egg on Easter Sunday was a way of celebrating the end of the period of fasting.
14. A certain Irish bishop allowed one biscuit to be taken with a cup of tea and an enterprising firm of confectioners in his diocese brought out a particularly large biscuit.
15. Pope Francis, *Evangelii Gaudium* (The Joy of the Gospel) (Dublin: Veritas, 2013), 120 (p. 66).

APPENDIX

The Continuity of Monastic Life in the Diocese of Waterford and Lismore

Early Foundations

The Diocese of Lismore and the Diocese of Waterford were set up by the Synod of Kells in 1152. They were united in 1363. The area covered by the united diocese had many religious foundations in the period before the twelfth century. The oldest at Ardmore was originally an episcopal centre established by St Declan. The largest was at Lismore, founded by St Carthage in the seventh century. It became a great centre of learning and played a significant role in the Twelfth-Century Reform. There were also monastic communities at Ardfinnan, founded by St Finnian the Leper, and at Clashmore, founded by St Mochua. The monasteries at Dairinis and Mothel continued into the sixteenth century and are mentioned below.

Monks and Canons Regular

The Benedictine Priory of St John in Waterford, founded in 1190, was dependent on the abbey of Bath in England. The community included monks and nuns who ran a hospital for the sick and poor of the city. At the time of the suppression in 1536 the community consisted of a prior, four brothers and three sisters.[1] The Cistercian Abbey of Inishlounaght near Clonmel, which had been founded from Mellifont in 1147, was suppressed in 1540.[2] The Cistercians would eventually return to the diocese when a group of Irish monks from the abbey of Melleray in Brittany would settle in the Knockmealdown Mountains in 1832, bringing the name of their motherhouse with them.

As in other parts of the country, the Augustinian canons regular were a significant presence in the diocese. Two of them represented earlier Irish monasteries that had been reconstituted as communities of canons regular in the twelfth century. These were Mothel Abbey, a few miles south of Carrick-on-Suir, the monastery of St Brogán and St Cuan founded in the sixth-century, and Molana Abbey, on an island near the mouth of the river Blackwater, which had been the sixth-century monastery of Dairinis founded by St Molanfide. Two others were founded in the early thirteenth century. These were Cahir Abbey and St Catherine's Abbey, Waterford. All four were suppressed between 1539 and 1541.[3]

Friars and Nuns

At the time of the dissolution there were several houses of mendicant friars in the Diocese of Waterford and Lismore. The Dominican Priory of St Saviour in Waterford, founded in 1226, was the earliest. The main Franciscan foundations were Waterford (1240), Clonmel (1269) and Carrickbeg (1336). There were also two rural Franciscan communities at Ardfinnan and at Curraheen near Aglish in West Waterford. The community at Ardfinnan was of the

Third Order and included married and single people. The community at Curraheen also included tertiaries.[4]

The Augustinian Friars had a priory at Abbeyside, Dungarvan, founded around 1290. Many of the medieval mendicant priories are referred to as abbeys, although, since the mendicants did not have abbots, their houses were not, strictly speaking, abbeys. The confusion may be the result of a mistranslation of the Irish *mainistir*.[5] Thus, Dún na Mainistreach was anglicised as Abbeyside.

The Carmelites did not have a strong presence in the Diocese of Waterford and Lismore, but there was a community of friars about a mile outside Ardfinnan, founded sometime after 1314.[6] The ruins of their church are still to be seen, but little is known about them.[7]

The three urban Franciscan houses were dissolved in 1540, while those of the Dominicans and Augustinian Friars were suppressed in 1541. The Ardfinnan Carmelites appear to have been suppressed the same year. The Ardfinnan Franciscans were dissolved in 1542, but the community in Curraheen seems to have been able to continue on quietly and became a place of refuge for the friars from Youghal.[8] The last Youghal friar died there in 1862.[9]

There were also communities of nuns. There was a convent of Poor Clares in Carrick-on-Suir, probably founded around the same time as the friary. It was suppressed in 1542. There was a very ancient community of nuns at Mollough near Newcastle on the Suir. Like many early Irish monasteries it may have adopted the Rule of St Augustine at some stage in its history. The last prioress was Mother Joan Power when the convent was suppressed in 1540.[10] It would be nearly three hundred years until monastic life for women would resume in the diocese with the founding of St Joseph's Carmelite Monastery in Tallow in 1836. Cistercian nuns made a foundation nearby at Glencairn in 1932.

In the Diocese of Waterford and Lismore the canons regular and the nuns seem to have disappeared in the aftermath of the dissolution. There were still a few Cistercians around for some time. Three monks received the abbatial blessing in 1625 including one for Inishlounaght and one for Mothel, although both these abbeys were in ruins and Mothel had not belonged to the Cistercians.[11]

Dominicans

The Dominicans had to leave Waterford following the suppression, but it appears that a number of them were living in hiding in rural parts of County Waterford. The trade between Waterford and Spain meant that young men aspiring to the priesthood could readily go to the continent to be trained. By the early 1600s a number of Waterford born Dominicans had returned to work in Ireland. By 1616 they were back in Waterford and by 1622 had a community of six. This was a period of growth for the Dominicans in Ireland. In the 1640s there were around four hundred members of the Order in the country. In 1642 they opened a house in Clonmel. The four members of the community there were martyred in 1650.[12]

In the 1660s and 1670s the Dominicans in Waterford were at times reduced to a single friar, but in 1687 they built a 'splendid chapel' within the city, possibly on the site of the present cathedral. They had to flee in 1698 when regular clergy were expelled from the country, but were back in 1713.[13] They helped with parochial work and preached in the parish chapels in the eighteenth century. These chapels or 'Mass-houses' as they were known, were simple thatched cabins with very basic furnishings. The Dominicans were also involved in education. Doctor Francis O'Finan OP, who later became bishop of Killala, lectured at the newly founded St John's College from 1807 to 1812. The college was set up by Bishop John Power to educate priests for Ireland and the Irish diaspora. The Dominicans closed their house in Waterford in 1832. From 1853 to 1865 the only member of the order living in Waterford was Fr Michael Joseph Moloney who celebrated Mass daily in the cathedral and was highly respected as a preacher.[14] In 1867 the priory was re-erected and the church in Bridge Street opened in 1877.[15] In 1975 the Dominicans took on responsibility for the newly created parish of St Saviour's, Ballybeg, in the suburbs of Waterford. The new parish church was dedicated to St Martin de Porres in 1981.[16]

Franciscans

Following the suppression, the Franciscans in Waterford went into hiding in Johnstown on the outskirts of the city. They opened an official residence there in 1612. They were forced to leave in 1652, but were able to return in 1660 and have maintained a presence in Waterford ever since. They did not have a public chapel until 1835, but prior to that helped the parish clergy in the simple Mass-houses of the eighteenth century.[17] The pattern was similar in Clonmel where the friars moved to Irishtown. Again they helped the parish clergy. They were able to return to the original site in 1828 and had the old friary restored and extended.[18]

In Carrick-on-Suir, where the friary was situated at St Molleran's in Carrickbeg, the friary was vacant for a hundred years until the Franciscans returned in 1644. This was a very troubled period during which the friars were in hiding most of the time. Blessed John Kearney was guardian of the community in Carrickbeg from 1649 until his martyrdom in Clonmel on 11 March 1653.[19] In 1669 the friars were able to return openly to the town.[20]

Augustinians

After the confiscation of their monastery in Abbeyside, the Augustinians in Dungarvan remained in the vicinity and may even have got some of their property back for a while in the 1590s. Throughout the seventeenth and eighteenth centuries they maintained a presence in the area, sometimes being hidden by sympathetic people in the nearby countryside.[21] A report to the government on the presence of religious houses in County Waterford in 1731 notes the presence of friars at Abbeyside (Augustinians) and Curraheen (Franciscans).[22]

In 1750 the Augustinians had a two-storey house at the Spring, about a mile to the west of Dungarvan, and they opened a Mass-house nearby shortly afterwards. In 1778 a novitiate was opened at the Spring.[23] In 1818 the friars closed the Mass-house at the Spring and opened a temporary chapel in a store in Church Street in the town. At the time they already had plans to build a proper church nearby. In 1829 St Augustine's Church on Friary Street was opened and the friars took up residence in the adjoining house on Main Street.[24] In 1972 a second Augustinian community was formed in the area when St Augustine's College, the secondary school run by the friars since 1874, moved from Main Street to the more spacious new facility at Duckspool, Abbeyside.[25]

Conclusion

The Carmelites, whose presence in the Diocese of Waterford and Lismore was small, did not re-establish themselves there after the dissolution of the monasteries. They did, however, continue in other parts of Ireland and had a continuous presence in the country during this time. I have dwelt on the survival and continuity of the other mendicants. They did not just survive. They helped the people to keep the faith. As part of that faith the Irish traditions of spirituality were handed on as well. There were also more recently founded religious orders whose members made an important contribution to the building up of the faith in Ireland. The Jesuits were particularly significant. They had houses in Waterford and Clonmel.[26] It is also worth noting that the secular clergy maintained their faithful service throughout the period.

NOTES

1. Cf. Dave Pollock, *Medieval Waterford, above and below ground* (Stradbally: Co. Waterford: Archeografix, 2014), p. 34.
2. Cf. Olden, op. cit., p. 9.
3. Cf. Olden, op. cit., p. 10.
4. Ibid.
5. *Mainistir*, monastery, from the Latin *monasterium*, *Muintir*, community, also derives from monasterium.
6. Cf. Ó Clabaigh, op. cit., p. 18.
7. Cf. Olden, op. cit., p. 10.
8. Ibid.
9. Cf. Patrick Conlan OFM, *Franciscan Ireland* (Cork: Mercier Press, 1978), p. 84.

10. Cf. Olden, op. cit., p. 11.
11. Cf. Olden, op. cit., p. 72.
12. Cf. Hugh Fenning OP, *The Dominicans in Waterford* (Waterford: Dominican Community, 1990), pp. 12–17.
13. Fenning, op. cit., pp. 17–23.
14. Fenning, op. cit., pp. 26–9.
15. Fenning, op. cit., pp. 30–3.
16. Fenning, op. cit., pp. 48–52.
17. Cf. Conlon, *Franciscan Ireland*, p. 105.
18. Ibid., p. 83.
19. Cf. Desmond Forristal, *Seventeen Martyrs* (Dublin: Columba Press, 1990), pp. 82–4.
20. Cf. Conlon, Franciscan Ireland, p. 80.
21. Thomas C. Butler, *Journey Of An Abbey 1292–1972 History of the Augustinians in Dungarvan* (Dublin: Good Counsel Press, 1973), pp. 8–12.
22. Butler, op. cit., p. 19.
23. Butler, op. cit., pp. 20–1.
24. Butler, op. cit., pp. 23–6.
25. Butler, op. cit., p. 53.
26. Olden, op. cit.